Case Studies in
Elementary and Secondary Curriculum

Case Studies in
Elementary and Secondary Curriculum

Marius Boboc | R. D. Nordgren
Cleveland State University

SAGE

Los Angeles | London | New Delhi
Singapore | Washington DC

For information:

SAGE Publications, Inc.
2455 Teller Road
Thousand Oaks, California 91320
E-mail: order@sagepub.com

SAGE Publications Ltd.
1 Oliver's Yard
55 City Road
London EC1Y 1SP
United Kingdom

SAGE Publications India Pvt. Ltd.
B 1/I 1 Mohan Cooperative Industrial Area
Mathura Road, New Delhi 110 044
India

SAGE Publications Asia-Pacific
 Pte. Ltd.
33 Pekin Street #02-01
Far East Square
Singapore 048763

Printed in the United States of America

Library of Congress Cataloging-in-Publication Data

Boboc, Marius.
  Case studies in elementary and secondary curriculum/Marius Boboc, R.D. Nordgren.
      p. cm.
  Includes bibliographical references and index.
  ISBN 978-1-4129-6055-7 (pbk.: alk. paper)
    1. Education, Elementary—Curricula—Case studies. 2. Education, Secondary—Curricula—Case studies. I. Nordgren, R. D., 1960- II. Title.

LB1570.B635 2010
373.19—dc22   2009025864

This book is printed on acid-free paper.

09   10   11   12   13   10 9   8   7   6   5   4   3   2   1

Acquisitions Editor:	Diane McDaniel
Editorial Assistant:	Ashley Conlon
Production Editor:	Brittany Bauhaus
Copy Editor:	Melinda Masson
Typesetter:	C&M Digitals (P) Ltd.
Proofreader:	Jeff Bryant
Indexer:	Diggs Publication Services, Inc.
Cover Designer:	Gail Buschman
Marketing Manager:	Christy Guilbault

Contents

Preface

On a daily basis, educators are faced with challenging situations that call for the implementation of problem-solving strategies that will help them overcome the situation at hand as well as possibly permanently change their practice. *Case Studies in Elementary and Secondary Curriculum* provides the reader with 21 cases in which educators from a variety of settings and representing different content areas are faced with a variety of curricular dilemmas. In some cases, they are able to solve the problem, while in others, they describe particular plans of action that they would implement. Some of the writers do not yet know the results of their responses for reasons that will become clear to the reader.

Over the years, our graduate students made us aware of a need for real-world examples that clarify the concept and relevance of curriculum—how it comes to life as a complex *process* or what *curriculum is* and *does* (Hyun, 2006). We see this process implying a continuum that ranges from design to implementation and evaluation. We should also note that this process needs constant analysis and change representing the essence of curriculum negotiations (Hyun, 2006). It is exactly that the implications of this process on one's student-centered professional practice were deemed a nagging concern by our graduate students, most of whom were practicing teachers. With this concern in mind, we have structured the book as a collection of case studies authored by individuals who, by day, teach students of all ages in a wide variety of settings and who, by night, are responsive and reflective graduate students. We are confident that you will relate to several aspects discussed in the case studies included for your analysis. The 21 qualitative case studies included in this text are particularistic in that each one of them places an emphasis on an individual "situation, event, program, or phenomenon"

(Merriam, 1998, p. 29). As you will see from the table of contents and the matrix provided later in this section, these case studies can be selected for your consideration by several criteria: (a) level—ranging from preschool to secondary; (b) most academic content areas; (c) setting—rural, suburban, and urban; and (d) emphasis—ranging from the level of individual classrooms to that of the school district. Additionally, we have included a set of elements—also called "spotlight on"—to be found across all educational settings as demonstrating "attributes of education" (Hewitt, 2006, p. 89). In this light, the selected case studies pose questions related to the interplay among pedagogy, instruction, curriculum, accountability, school reform, support, and leadership, with a myriad of correlations that could be made to discrete components of what defines teaching and learning in today's increasingly complex educational settings.

CASE STUDY TOPICS

In our contemporary schools, finding a curricular problem along the stage of design, implementation, or evaluation is not a difficult task. The case study authors had to go through a reflective process in order to identify relevant curricular issues impacting their professional practice and propose manageable solutions to them. For instance, Case Study 2 relates to the proactive role a teacher has to play as a way to address the current issue of school financing by means of community engagement. In comparison, Case Study 5 grounds curriculum adaptations and skill-building remedial work in the context of standards-based education.

We are well aware of the great range of changes to what curriculum is and what it does at any level of educational settings. This constitutes the main reason for which we have included case studies developed around whole-school and districtwide curricular problems. In this light, of special concern to our students are the mandates that accompany the accountability movement: standards, testing, and curriculum alignment. Often they challenge a teacher's ability to implement his or her curriculum based on creativity and a genuine focus on what each student should actually be learning. At the same time, we want to promote meaningful conversations about curricular design and decision making that lead to "new knowledge construction that empowers learners, teachers, and others" (Hyun, 2006, p. 22). We hope that the inclusion of case studies addressing a wide range of curricular issues will give you hope and inspire you to make changes that you feel are practical, ethical, and participatory to all those involved.

THE USE OF CASE STUDIES

Most of us are aware that college textbooks—chock full of philosophies, theories, and strategies organized and described in varying degrees of clarity—cannot provide us with all the knowledge and skills necessary to be successful practitioners. While supplying us with a great amount of information, they too often lack the personal voices that are necessary for connections between theory and practice to occur. By using authentic voices, consumers of such specialized texts can establish a connection to the practical side of teaching where we are encouraged to tap into our personal teaching philosophies, examine the theories learned in our various coursework, and apply the strategies we have gained from a myriad of sources: textbooks, workshops, observations, or our own schooling experiences. Encompassing this process we use reflection and responsiveness as guiding principles for effective teaching.

We believe the voices heard in this book will place the reader into the shoes of each of these teacher authors, allowing for an immersion in "the complexities, ambiguities, and uncertainties" (Golich, Boyer, Franko, & Lamy, 2000, p. 1) of their situation while finding a personal response to the problem that is directly or indirectly inhibiting their teaching and, consequently, their students' learning. The rationale behind the particularistic case selection proposed by the current text aims at providing the audience with opportunities to "achieve competence" (Flyvbjerg, 2006, p. 222) in deconstructing issues affecting curriculum as it is negotiated by teachers in "its real-life context" (Yin, 1994, p. 13) of their "local schools and communities" (Koballa & Tippins, 2000, p. 3).

Traditionally speaking, the structure of a case study introduces the reader to a context within which a particular problem occurs, followed by the actual description of the problem in question, and, finally, by a set of questions for the audience. The purpose of this set of questions is to attempt to resolve the problem at hand by asking for someone else's opinion on the matter. While readers are left with an almost endless array of solutions that may or may not address the problem described in the case study, there is no actual manner in which to check on the validity of any of these reader-generated solutions. This can be disconcerting to those of us who are analytical in nature, but we must come to understand what can be gained by gathering a great number of possible solutions: One of these can, with a little adaptation, become the key to a serious curricular problem.

Many of us have spent a great deal of time in graduate classes using case studies as a discussion anchor. While the tool itself provides us with a wealth of information correlated to both theories and practical applications we bring to such classes, we may take away a rather convenient solution to the problem elaborated in a case study. This is the turning point in our thinking about the format of the case studies included in this book. In addition to the elements of our standard case study format (background information, curriculum information, exposition of the associated problem or problems, and probing questions), these case studies allow you to confront real-life curricular concerns that require you to *tie theory to practice*. The extra elements that strengthen such connections focus on having each author propose a solution to his or her own curricular problem. In several instances, the practitioners are able to analyze the validity of their proposal by outlining a set of "observed outcomes" as a result of the implementation of the "actual solution." In other instances, we are dealing with proposals aimed at resolving the given problem. Along the same lines, each proposed solution is followed by a set of expected outcomes. The ensuing reflection makes a stronger case for the connection between theory and practice, mediated through each case study.

Despite a mandated format, the voices differ from study to study as each author has his or her own story to tell and his or her own way of telling it. Personalization is clear. We know that the most compelling information is often supplied to us through narrative, and it is our intent that the lessons learned by these teachers will indeed be compelling to you. It is our hope that these studies will persuade you to make changes in your practice and how you think about the science and art of teaching.

While we would expect that all teachers reading this book will have already gained the experience necessary to chip away at the "several thousand" cases Flyvbjerg (2006, p. 222) says are necessary to become an expert practitioner, we believe it to be quite valuable for all to begin thinking like researchers, especially case study researchers. These case studies will allow you to do just that. Rather than exposing you to theories of curriculum and instruction in your textbooks and coursework and then asking you to correctly identify their need or use on a test or paper, we prompt you to shift to "application mode." Our "points to ponder" pertaining to each case will engage you into synthesis and analysis modes. One example of such prompts is provided by the following questions pertinent to one of our case studies: "How should teachers within the same school tackle the task of creating a curriculum revision team? Would you use Walker's deliberative approach? What procedural steps would you want to see in place as a result of this forming process?" Questions such as these address the call for teachers to do more than apply techniques in their classroom but allow them to "reason through dilemmas, investigate problems, and analyze student learning to develop appropriate curriculum for a diverse group of learners" as advocated by Darling-Hammond, Hammerness, Grossman, Rust, and Shulman (2005, p. 392) in their call to redesign teacher education programs. We must profoundly believe and continually demonstrate that we are reflective and responsive practitioners who can and do identify problems, collect data, analyze those data, and change our practice to rectify those problems.

ORGANIZATION AND FEATURES

Each study uses the following format by describing these components:

- **Background Information About the Teacher**
- **Background Information About the Curriculum**
- **Problem** (emphasizing any combination of the "attributes of education" mentioned earlier)
- **Probing Questions**

You'll find that each author has a unique background and set of experiences, yet we're confident you'll be able to relate to each of them even if your current situation and future teaching plans don't coincide with theirs.

Although "curriculum" seems to mean different things to different people, we would like you to define it by connecting your previous knowledge with the curricular "episodes" described by the case studies included in this book. Once you have identified what curriculum *is,* you can focus your attention on what curriculum *does,* as a way to deconstruct the various factors influencing its negotiations in the professional practice of our teacher authors. To that end, we offer 21 different curricular problems and nearly as many curricula. These allow you to make connections between the curriculum and instruction theory learned in your coursework and "reality," which is what can happen across all contexts of practice.

We would also like to emphasize the use of *text boxes* in the body of several case studies as an effective way to provide the readers with some brief background information related to an important element in the analysis of the given case study.

In addition to the five sections listed and described above, we offer two more features:

- **Proposed/Actual Solution**
- **Expected/Observed Outcomes**

The reason for which some of the solutions are "proposed" is that often the teachers/authors don't have the resources to implement their solutions to the problems. This is quite problematic but common for teachers, as you're well aware, as we are often disempowered by the administration, school, and/or system to make the changes necessary for success. Nevertheless, these solutions are informed attempts at solving their respective curricular problems—think of them as action research projects undertaken to improve one's pedagogical practice. The "expected" outcomes represent opportunities to evaluate the decisions made by our practitioners. In cases where our authors had a chance to implement an actual solution, the latter section focuses on "observed" outcomes.

These two sections of each study allow you to "check in" with the authors in an attempt to validate the solutions discussed in your college classroom or as a home assignment. We have designed the presentation of each study so that you are left with probing questions, to determine for yourself how best to solve the dilemma or dilemmas presented. You can then, as an individual or as part of a community of learners, compare your answer to what actually did happen or what the authors determined would work (and is supported by the editors). We acknowledge that most problems have more than one viable solution, so the ones provided by the authors are not necessarily the best or only ways to resolution. We invite you to adapt these situations to the specificities of your practice. By changing the environment, the solution may need to be altered. We believe this to be self-evident as we take you through these 21 case studies.

The last section in the structure of our collection of practitioner-written, particularistic case studies offers the audience opportunities to meta-analyze their curriculum knowledge and skills, as demonstrated by the following features:

POINTS TO PONDER . . .

Each case study concludes with a set of open-ended questions representing an invitation for readers to elaborate further on how the solution proposed by the case study author may unfold or on how it may impact other curricular levels than the one representing the base for the case study in question.

QUESTIONS FOR SCHOOL ADMINISTRATORS

As we strongly believe in the complex responsibility of being an effective instructional leader in today's schools, we want to include such professionals in any curriculum-based conversations generated by each case study. Reviewing these questions by both administrators and teachers would open up communication channels designed to "lead" schools into meeting the 21st-century requirements.

IN-CLASS EXERCISE

In an attempt to provide our audience with opportunities for synthesis, each case study incorporates a suggested collaborative exercise aimed at applying analytical skills to situations that are familiar to teachers and administrators alike. Under these circumstances, the in-class exercise is a logical continuation of the focus on a particular curricular problem described in the case study.

SUGGESTED READINGS

All case studies include several recommended readings, which help contextualize particular curricular problems and their solutions representing the core of our collaborative work.

THE CASE STUDIES' AUTHORS

As noted earlier, the authors are all practicing teachers in various graduate programs at a state university with an explicit focus on increasingly diverse educational settings. Despite the latter, many of these authors do not practice in cities but are oftentimes in affluent suburban enclaves, far from the problems and concerns specific to city schools. However, their problems are just as serious to their practice as those that confront their urban colleagues. Undoubtedly, you will notice these differences and will likely relate to each author based on your own schooling experiences.

We consulted each author after the initial submission of a study, asking him or her to provide further details of different aspects of the study, especially updates on the implementation of the solution. These updates and, on some occasions, revisions were made and added to the study.

THE CASE STUDY MATRIX (p. xvii)

The book is arranged so that you can easily access case studies that pertain to a wide range of content areas (English-language arts, mathematics, science, social studies, modern languages, art, special education, etc.), grade levels (preschool to high school), educational settings (rural, suburban, and urban), and topics that relate your interest in curriculum theory in your graduate-level coursework. A case study matrix has been provided to help you select cases for analysis and discussion. We're confident, however, that you will also enjoy and benefit from reading the book from cover to cover because, as we mentioned earlier, you will no doubt make personal connections to the authors of all our studies.

REFERENCES

Darling-Hammond, L., Hammerness, K., Grossman, P., Rust, F., & Shulman, L. (2005). The design of teacher education programs. In L. Darling-Hammond & J. Bransford, Eds., *Preparing teachers for a changing world: What teachers should learn and be able to do* (pp. 390–441). San Francisco: Jossey-Bass.

Flyvbjerg, B. (2006). Five misunderstandings about case-study research. *Qualitative Inquiry, 12*(2), 219–245.

Golich, V. L., Boyer, M., Franko, P., & Lamy, S. (2000). *The ABCs of case teaching.* Washington, DC: Institute for the Study of Diplomacy.

Hewitt, T. W. (2006). *Understanding and shaping curriculum: What we teach and why.* Thousand Oaks, CA: Sage.

Hyun, E. (2006). *Teachable moments: Re-conceptualizing curricula understandings.* New York: Peter Lang Publishing, Inc.

Koballa, T. R., & Tippins, D. J. (2000). *Cases in middle and secondary science education: The promise and dilemmas.* Upper Saddle River, NJ: Merrill/Prentice Hall.

Merriam, S. B. (1998). *Qualitative research and case study applications in education.* San Francisco: Jossey-Bass.

Yin, R. K. (1994). *Case study research: Design and methods* (2nd ed.) Thousand Oaks, CA: Sage.

Acknowledgments

The authors would like to thank all of our former students who contributed to this work. We thoroughly enjoyed revisiting these studies and reconnecting with these exceptional practitioners.

Julie Babcock

Christy Bauer

Brandie Bischel

James Stoddard Dare

Amy Derethik

Lori Elgin

April Foster

Elana Gazella

Marlena Gill

Lindsay Herwerden

Tracy Johnson

Julie Keller

Maryjane Kubach

Jenny Moran

Kim Nealy

Patricia Neligan

Lynn Nock

Valentina Sulaj

Corinne Thibault

Mae Thorpe

J. A. Williams

We would also like to express gratitude to the reviewers listed below. Without their constructive criticism and words of encouragement, this book would not have been possible.

Phyllis A. Gimbel, *Bridgewater State College*

Burnette Wolf Hamil, *Mississippi State University*

Theresa Harris, *Coppin State University*

John D. Hunt, *Mississippi College*

Barbara Gonzalez Pino, *University of Texas at San Antonio*

William Rieck, *University of Louisiana at Lafayette*

Amany Saleh, *Arkansas State University*

L. E. Steinmetz, *University of Texas at San Antonio*

Frances van Tassell, *University of North Texas*

Marsh Zenanko, *Jacksonville State University*

Finally, we would like to thank Diane McDaniel and Ashley Conlon for their undying support of this project.

Case Study Matrix

Title	Brief Description	Spotlight on	Level	Content Area	Setting	Page Number
1. Bringing Diversity Into a Less Diverse Environment	Investigating possible ways to enhance the planned/designed curriculum by incorporating multicultural themes/topics, leading to increased awareness of multiculturalism in the larger, less diverse community	Inclusion of multicultural themes/topics into the planned/designed curriculum	High school	Social studies	Rural	1
2. Bringing Calculus to Life: Hands-on Learning in a New Sequence of Courses	Identifying means by which to incorporate more hands-on instructional methods into the taught curriculum, while considering the latter's selection of scope and sequence based on students' prior knowledge and experience	a) Incorporation of hands-on instructional strategies into the taught curriculum b) Selection of scope and sequence of planned curriculum	High school	Mathematics	Suburban	7
3. Meeting the Individual Needs of Each Student at an Alternative High School	Enhancing the planned curriculum by making decisions based on data coming from three sources of information—context, content, and students—designed to restructure a set of independent learning packets	Enhancement and restructuring of planned curriculum	High school	English-language arts	Urban	15

(Continued)

(Continued)

Title	Brief Description	Spotlight on . . .	Level	Content Area	Setting	Page Number
4. Using Assessment and Student Interest Data to Inform Differentiated Instruction in an Inclusive Classroom	Bridging the gap between students' aptitudes and standards-based instruction by means of preassessment and differentiation interdisciplinary	a) Quantification of students' knowledge and skills in the content area b) Identification and provision of support to meet students' needs based on enhanced awareness of their background	Middle school	Mathematics	Urban	23
5. Motivating Students to Learn in a Peer-Supported School Environment	Identifying appropriate means to motivate students by going beyond peer observations and constructive criticism in an environment adhering to principles of differentiated instruction	a) Student choices in learning b) Sustainable student engagement in learning activities	Kindergarten	English-language arts (reading)	Urban	31
6. Authentic Audience and Affective Learning in a Gifted and Talented Middle School Program	Engaging in interdisciplinary planning as way to integrate content in a middle school gifted and talented program by connecting the affective domain and "authentic audiences"	a) Gifted and talented learners b) Affective learning c) Teachable moments d) Authentic learning e) Content integration	Middle school	All core subjects	Suburban	39
7. "Discovery Math": From Professional Development to Classroom Practice	Improving the implementation and feedback loop of districtwide professional development opportunities designed to disseminate information about new content-area pedagogies	Professional development	School district	Mathematics	Urban, suburban, and rural	47

(Continued)

xix

Title	Brief Description	Spotlight on . . .	Level	Content Area	Setting	Page Number
12. Prevention Programs as Means to Teach Social Skills in Elementary School	Integrating social skills into the planned curriculum by implementing a schoolwide program engaging students in regular interactions designed to increase their awareness of a particular set of skills	a) Social skills b) Hidden curriculum c) Special education	Elementary school	N/A	Suburban	85
13. Educating the Community About a Needed Levy Increase: The Teacher as a Political Activist	Articulating a teacher's emerging leadership skills beyond the classroom to engage the larger community in supporting the school by means of a levy	a) Engaging community b) Role of teacher beyond the classroom	Districtwide	N/A	Inner-ring suburban	93
14. The Mandated Curriculum Meeting the Needs of Teachers and Their Favored Practices	Finding a balance between a newly mandated curriculum and the existing curriculum practices emphasizes a gradual implementation accompanied by frequent evaluation of effectiveness based on student engagement and performance levels	a) Mandated curriculum b) Teacher autonomy c) Accountability	Elementary school	English-language arts	Suburban	99
15. Balancing Data-Driven Decision Making and Shifting Paradigms in a New Elementary Math Curriculum	Providing teachers with appropriate resources to ensure an effective implementation of a new curriculum designed to address deficiencies in student performance indicated by previous assessment data	a) Implementation of a districtwide curriculum b) Accountability requirements	Elementary school	Mathematics	Urban/ suburban	107
16. Professional Development That Works, Please!	Designing districtwide professional development opportunities given a tougher fiscal environment and an apparent lack of interest from potential participating teachers	Professional development	School district	All core subjects	Urban/ suburban	115

Bringing Diversity Into a Less Diverse Environment

Prereading Focus Points: The teacher investigates possible ways to expand his planned/designed curriculum by incorporating multicultural themes/topics. The direct implications of the taught curriculum derive from the identification and selection of instructional methods designed to promote student interest in these themes/topics, particularly given the circumstances of the teaching context and its larger community. Consequently, the teacher also ponders the issue of the transfer of multiculturalism-focused knowledge and skills into the community. One specific area of interest is community support and family involvement as a means to validate the choice for the multicultural themes/topics.

Level: High school

Content Area: Social studies

Setting: Rural

Spotlight on . . . Inclusion of multicultural themes/topics in the curriculum

Key Terms: Tolerance; stereotypes

BACKGROUND INFORMATION ABOUT THE TEACHER

Jared has been a high school social studies teacher for 6 years, all of which were spent in two different small, rural school districts in two Midwestern states. He graduated from a university in the same region of the country in December 1999 with a secondary education degree, a major in history, and a minor in social studies.

Jared entered college as a history major and during his sophomore year decided to pursue a teaching career. He was unsure about that decision until he entered his internship, and from that point on he knew he had made the correct decision. During his career he has taught U.S. history, world history, American government, world geography, integrated social studies, sociology, and psychology. In addition to teaching, he serves as a coach for girls' volleyball and boys' track and field.

Jared's current school, Hillside Senior High School, is located in a small town in the northeast corner of a Midwestern state. The school serves approximately 400 students, grades 10 through 12. It is a homogenous culture, as less than 1% of the student population is considered minority. The students are Caucasian, either Catholic or Baptist. Class size varies, with the average about 25 students per class. At this time, the graduation rate is 90%, including students who graduated from alternative forms of education.

The town itself could be classified as relatively self-sufficient. There is a small business sector in town and a local hospital. The majority of workers are either farmers or manual laborers. As a result, the majority of students come from working-class families, with little post–high school education. The number of single-parent households is quite high, and drug and alcohol abuse is a rampant problem among high school students. The community seems to be welcoming of those of similar heritage, but the same may not be said as far as ethnic minorities are concerned. Although it is predominately dormant, Jared has been informed that there is a local Ku Klux Klan chapter in the county. However, the neighboring community is renowned for its ethnic diversity, representing Mexican American, Jewish, and many Eastern European cultures.

BACKGROUND INFORMATION ABOUT THE CURRICULUM

The state does not have a standardized curriculum, which allows individual school districts to develop their own curricula. That seems to promote curriculum development designed to flexibly meet student needs. Yet, with the No Child Left Behind Act (NCLB) in place, the reality is centered on accountability requirements expected to be met by the use of the State Test for Education Development (STED).

The school administration places a heavy emphasis on STED scores. The community judges the effectiveness of the school and teachers on the results of the test. As a result, the curriculum has become goal-oriented. School board policy mandates that all teachers should post their lesson plans online. Additionally, all teachers have to document how those lessons meet curricular requirements. In Jared's first year teaching at Hillside, the district purchased new textbooks for the social studies department. The textbooks that were chosen aligned with the national benchmarks. The rationale for this decision was that these textbooks would prepare students for the STED.

However, the district intentionally developed the social studies curriculum to focus on big ideas, such as citizenship, technology, reading comprehension, writing skills, and communication. The curriculum allows for flexibility in terms of when and how these big ideas will be taught. For example, in 11th-grade U.S. history, Jared focuses primarily on the 20th century and the development of modern America. The other history teacher spends much more time on the late 19th century. Those two classes are not aligned chronologically, but they still follow the guidelines of the planned/designed curriculum.

PROBLEM

As a social studies teacher, Jared needs to provide opportunities for his students to discuss the wealth of diversity and its consequent impact on the American culture. Considering the wide range of microcultures that make up our diverse American culture in the 21st century (Banks, 2004), Jared thinks it is his responsibility to prepare students for responsible citizenship, with a focus on multiculturalism. Under these circumstances, it would be a matter of identifying ways in which to effectively teach diversity and the contributions of minority groups to the American society in an isolated, homogenous community. The building blocks to knowledge do not exist as his students possess little to no background experience with ethnic, religious, racial, or sexual minorities. The town is a relatively isolated community; consequently, mass media may be its only source of information related to such minority groups. Furthermore, the town does not have any educational resources to institute a multicultural curriculum. Finally, Jared is faced with the dilemma of altering the curriculum in a manner that might not directly meet the demands of the STED or NCLB.

PROBING QUESTIONS

1. How might multiculturalism be incorporated into the planned/designed curriculum in ways that appeal to both students and the community?

2. How might the students' families be included in teaching tolerance and challenging stereotypes so as not to create tension between school and home?

> **Tolerance** is the ability to accept ideas, viewpoints, perspectives, or practices different from one's own.

PROPOSED SOLUTION

1. According to Banks (2004), the teacher must feel comfortable and knowledgeable in order to motivate students. Therefore, Jared has to be cognizant of the multicultural construction of American society in an attempt to justify to the administration and parents the importance and relevance of multicultural education in the community.

One of the flaws of the planned/designed curriculum is that it does not present contributions of minority groups in a cohesive, integrated manner. Banks (2004) uses the example of only mentioning African Americans during Black History Month. Hillside's social studies textbook falls into this trap by highlighting only one minority per chapter. Instead, by presenting curriculum in a flexible manner that implies high levels of student interactions with the curriculum materials, Jared could help students understand that culture is a combination of all ethnic groups. For example, if Jared's students were to do a reverse study of the history of popular music, they could see all the contributions made over the past century. They could start with today's popular music—rap, country and western, and rock—and trace their developments back to turn-of-the-century jazz in the South. Students would understand that many ethnic groups have contributed to the popular music they know and like today and that modern-day rap and country and western are related. Once students have grasped this concept, they could investigate the origins of other multicultural aspects of the American culture.

> **Stereotypes** are labels or categories applied to individuals identifying as belonging to a particular group, thus leading to isolation or discrimination.

2. Sparking students' interest in multiculturalism would be closely tied to integrating their families into the curriculum. Most of the students feel the issue has nothing to do with them. Jared needs to create awareness- and empathy-building activities to help them understand the complex issues of diversity and tolerance. For instance, he could create situations where each student is a minority based on any number of features such as hair, eyes, clothes, or height. Based on these trait-based groups, students would interact with one another (across groups) in ways that are not as inclusive as they are used to, thus giving them an idea of exclusion and its affective toll on individuals. In parallel, students would be engaged in designing interviewing protocols involving their family members, from which they can complete a family genealogy. Students would discover their ethnic heritage, after which they would research their ethnicity and discover how their ancestors were treated by society. The final step would then be to find out about the various contributions

their culture made to the United States. Thus they would discover the active role their families played in the fabric of American culture and learn from each other. In an attempt to extend the impact of this multi-cultural awareness–raising activity, students could share their findings, in a format chosen by each one of them, with a live audience made up of family and community members, thus allowing for an exchange of ideas after the student presentations.

Once Jared is able to implement and evaluate these changes to his planned/designed curriculum, his next task would have to involve the school's other social studies teacher in initiating preliminary talks about expanding the process he uses. Along the way, school administration would have to be informed as a way to seek assistance in identifying resources that would render these schoolwide efforts effective. As findings emerge from the whole process, Jared and his colleagues could investigate appropriate ways in which to disseminate relevant information to the larger community. For example, the school could host a multicultural fair as part of the school year opening ceremonies.

EXPECTED OUTCOMES

By restructuring his planned/designed curriculum to include aspects related to multiculturalism, Jared hopes to achieve three main goals. First, students' motivation and interest would increase by their investigation and research into their own heritage, intertwining family, community, and the greater American culture. Second, once students have gained an understanding of their role in society, they would recognize that the United States is a multicultural nation and all groups influence the shared culture. This would lead to increased tolerance, as well as the knowledge that the U.S. culture is continually evolving with the influence of diversity. Finally, over time and by constant involvement in school activities, the viewpoints of the community would change and become more accepting, as stereotypes would be gradually broken down.

POINTS TO PONDER . . .

Imagine you are teaching in a small community where there is not a lot of diversity. How would you initiate any conversation with your colleagues and/or school administration about a prospective plan of action designed to increase awareness and develop knowledge about multiculturalism? What would you do to accommodate these efforts by curricular changes that you could make? How would you engage the larger community in the process?

QUESTIONS FOR ADMINISTRATORS

Given the fact that there is no curriculum mandated by the state, how would you be able to support Jared's efforts to infuse multiculturalism into the social studies curriculum? How would you coordinate appropriate plans to engage the community in raising awareness about diversity in a rather homogeneous environment? What type of rewards system would you create to sustain such collaborative work done in your school?

IN-CLASS ACTIVITY

Form groups that have at least one person teaching social studies (this would be a preferred composition). In these groups, discuss the elements of an action plan that Jared could use to inform the district about his efforts to enhance his curriculum with activities and materials designed to increase student and community awareness about diversity. Create a T-chart outlining some of the problems (on one side of the T) as well as facilitators (on the other side of the T) Jared might encounter in his efforts to initiate a bottom-up approach to curriculum development at the level of his school district.

REFERENCE

Banks, J. A. (2004). Multicultural education: Characteristics and goals. In J. A. Banks & C. A. McGee Banks (Eds.), *Multicultural education: Issues and perspectives* (5th ed., pp. 3–26). Hoboken, NJ: Wiley.

SUGGESTED READINGS

Banks, J. A. (2003). *Teaching strategies for ethnic studies* (7th ed.). Boston: Allyn & Bacon.

Banks, J. A., & Banks, C. A. M. (Eds.). (2004). *Handbook of research on multicultural education* (2nd ed.). San Francisco: Jossey-Bass.

Cyrus, V. (Ed.). (1999). *Experiencing race, class, and gender in the United States* (3rd ed.). New York: McGraw-Hill.

Delpit, L., & Dowdy, J. K. (Eds.). (2002). *The skin that we speak: Thoughts on language and culture in the classroom.* New York: New Press.

Gay, G. (2000). *Culturally responsive teaching: Theory, research, and practice.* New York: Teachers College Press.

Bringing Calculus to Life

Hands-on Learning in a New Sequence of Courses

Prereading Focus Points: On the one hand, the teacher probes into appropriate ways in which the planned/designed curriculum could translate into a taught curriculum that incorporates more hands-on instructional methods designed to improve student participation, motivation, and performance. On the other hand, there is a larger issue of the selection of scope and sequence of the planned/designed curriculum based on the students' prior knowledge and experience in terms of the content area.

Level: High school

Content Area: Mathematics

Setting: Suburban

Spotlight on...

    a) Incorporation of hands-on instructional strategies into the taught curriculum; and
    b) Selection of scope and sequence of planned/design curriculum.

Key Terms: Advanced Placement courses; multiple intelligences; curriculum mapping

BACKGROUND INFORMATION ABOUT THE TEACHER

Lee has been teaching high school mathematics for 24 years at Excelsior High School after returning to the profession when her youngest child began school. She has taught students at all levels of mathematics. Presently she is teaching a new course—Non–Advanced Placement Calculus—in the mathematics department.

She graduated from a state university with a major in mathematics and a minor in education. Her curriculum course consisted of some curriculum content but was mostly a crash course in the "new math" that she would have to teach but never actually studied in her schooling. Her lesson plans are based on knowing what content to cover as written in department "courses of study" and using her own ideas of how best to teach it. She attended many workshops and conventions and learned some very useful techniques to use in the past courses that she taught.

Excelsior High School is an all-girls' college preparatory parochial school in a large city suburb with a little over 20,000 people. The school district has four public schools and six private schools. Students come from more than 50 public, private, and parochial coeducational grade schools. About half begin their study of math at Excelsior High School with Algebra 1 and the other half with Geometry or Honors Geometry.

BACKGROUND INFORMATION ABOUT THE CURRICULUM

The mathematics curriculum for each course is stated in terms of student outcomes. The teacher, as a subject matter specialist, is responsible for selecting and organizing learning experiences and evaluating their effectiveness. Much of this is done by more or less following the selected text. New texts—purchased on an average of every 5 years—provide many teaching supplements to help in lesson planning.

Courses are arranged in the traditional sequence with both "honors" and "regular" sections except for Algebra 1, which has no honors counterpart. There is one remedial course, Math 3, for juniors. There are three Advanced Placement courses: Calculus AB, Calculus BC, and Statistics. Eighty-nine percent of the senior class is enrolled in their fourth year of mathematics. Ninety percent of students pass the mathematics section of the state graduation test on the first try. This is done with minimal specific preparation—occasional review in the weeks prior to the test. For those who do not pass, after-school remediation is provided.

Specific courses and their curricula are determined by members of the mathematics department with oversight by the administrator responsible for curriculum development. National Council of Teachers of Mathematics (NCTM) standards are addressed in the curriculum, and all teachers are committed to their implementation. There is no standard evaluation to determine if teachers teach and students learn the written curriculum. Teachers are autonomous in their classes.

Advanced Placement (AP) courses represent college-bound, content-driven curricula for students who demonstrate the required level of cognitive performance.

The students taking the non-AP calculus course are students who have not been in the honors sequence in mathematics or have chosen to leave the honors sequence. They studied precalculus in their junior year, and previous to the 2006–2007 school year, they had only an AP statistics course or a semester-long statistics and probability course to select as a senior math course. After much discussion in the mathematics department, this course was proposed. The course curriculum is based loosely on the AP curriculum, as it was felt that "calculus is calculus." Therefore, Lee is faced with the problem of finding methods to instruct students in order to understand the concepts of calculus and go beyond manipulation skills to apply calculus concepts in problem solving. At the same time, a larger issue seems to be related to deciding whether this calculus course is the best choice for these students or whether there is a more appropriate course for nonhonors students to take after studying precalculus.

PROBING QUESTIONS

1. How might the concepts of calculus—and not just the manipulation skills that the students seem to expect from a mathematics course—be taught effectively?

2. How might problem solving, an area usually disliked by students and often relegated to a minor place in most math classes because of the students' lack of success in this area and the emphasis most courses place on manipulation skills, be taught effectively?

3. Is there another course that might be more appropriate for students who have not been in Honors Precalculus?

PROPOSED SOLUTION

1. Since calculus is the study of change, technology that allows for visualization of the fluidity involved in the concepts is needed. Geometer's Sketchpad is an example of interactive software that allows students to explore calculus concepts involving change. Lessons built around the diagrams that can be put "into motion" can have a great impact on student understanding and long-term retention of information. Also,

teacher-created, Web-based demonstrations of calculus concepts—for example, http://www.stewartcalculus.com/media/3_home.php and http://www.ies.co.jp/math/products/calc/menu.html—could be incorporated into lessons.

Using pencils, paper, and graphing calculators in discovery activities can help in understanding the need for "speeding up" the tedious traditional calculations by using calculus to arrive at problem solutions. These types of activities take valuable class time but are worth the effort if students understand what functionality calculus has in solving problems.

By using varying strategies in presenting calculus concepts, students would use multiple modalities (thus employing multiple intelligences) in learning calculus. Even though mathematics teachers have always used visual diagrams along with verbal explanation, adding motion visuals and activities in which they have to create the diagrams should help in this area.

2. Lee tells her students that there is no reason to learn the manipulations of calculus if they are not able to use those skills to apply the concepts of calculus in problem solving. Problem solving is given lip service in all courses of study. Most of the time is spent on teaching manipulation skills. Therefore, in this course, Lee needs to teach problem-solving strategies in general and then have students analyze problems that can be solved using calculus and apply calculus concepts to real-world problem situations. Business, the social sciences, and the life sciences all use calculus, and usually students majoring in these areas require a course in calculus in college.

> **Multiple intelligences** are the core of a theory generated by Gardner (1983), as he claimed that IQ scores alone cannot reveal an individual's true set of abilities.

Interdisciplinary units with physics and economics classes, interactive laboratory activities, and videos depicting the applications of calculus in the real world could all benefit the understanding of the applications of calculus. Dewey (1900/1990) stated that education and schools should model and benefit society in general. Problem solving in a group project setting would better model the way problem situations are addressed in the larger communities we find ourselves. As Ayers (2001) writes, we need to liberate the curriculum from doing the same thing over and over. We need to engage our students' interests. We have been caught up in the idea that every student has to experience the same curriculum. But doing problem solving in a group situation with each group becoming knowledgeable about applications in one field (instead of all students doing all types of problems) will still result in the student seeing that calculus has applications and will develop her problem-solving abilities.

3. Nel Noddings (1994) feels that the math curriculum in high schools should meet the needs and interests of the students. Excelsior High School is college preparatory and has a 3-year mathematics requirement. Most students elect to take 4 years of math. All students take math through Algebra 2 (a requirement of all colleges), and the students who begin with Geometry take Precalculus as their third year of math. Most of these students want to take a fourth year, and the question remains: What is the best course to offer these students? Is Calculus the only choice because it is what traditionally comes next?

Research will need to be done in an attempt to answer the following probing questions Lee would use to engage her colleagues:

a) What are other comparable schools offering their students in this situation, and what are their outcomes?
b) How satisfied are students with the calculus course, and what do they feel they need in a fourth-year math course?
c) What textbooks are available to use in a "mathematical applications" or "advanced mathematical concepts" type of course? Might this fulfill the needs expressed by the students?

EXPECTED OUTCOMES

If Lee uses dynamic visuals and provides hands-on activities, her students should understand better the basic concepts of calculus. The idea that calculus is the study of change, while algebra is static in nature, is difficult to grasp. By observing demonstrations of this fluidity, students should be able to use more of their learning styles in gaining this understanding.

Students would come from a study of calculus applications with enhanced problem-solving skills and an appreciation of the uses of calculus. They may not think of mathematics as only a set of rote manipulations to do in response to a set of exercises. Applications to real-world situations should be the goal of the study of mathematics.

Determining the best course to offer students in their fourth year of mathematics would benefit students by providing a class designed to engage both students who may end their study of mathematics in high school and those who may study more mathematics in college. No matter what course is offered, problem solving should be a major component of that course. Ayers (2001) states, "I believe that the purpose of school is to open doors, open worlds, and open possibilities for each person to live life fully and well" (p. 60).

POINTS TO PONDER . . .

How would you collaboratively "map the curriculum" (in any content area) to determine the prerequisite knowledge and skills that students should have in order to be successful in a sequence of courses in one given academic discipline? What choices would you offer students based on the various ability levels they demonstrate at the beginning of the sequence of courses in question? Under these circumstances, how would you accommodate student transience?

> **Curriculum mapping** is a complex process by which curricula are analyzed in terms of how their sequence over the academic calendar correlates with student learning assessment data.

QUESTIONS FOR ADMINISTRATORS

Stemming from the apparent belief that "calculus is calculus" (here you could replace "calculus" with any other content area), how would you get your teachers in a given academic discipline to "rethink" their own pedagogical content knowledge as a way to increase student performance and reveal real-life applications to motivate learners? As a school leader, how would you model any kind of "thinking outside the box" leading to innovations in teaching and learning?

IN-CLASS ACTIVITY

In content/discipline area groups, discuss how you would put together a district-level set of professional development opportunities designed around project-based learning. Prepare an oral presentation of your group consensus. Make sure to emphasize any follow-up plans meant to prompt the implementation of any "lessons learned" during these professional development opportunities.

REFERENCES

Ayers, W. (2001). *To teach: The journey of a teacher* (2nd ed.). New York: Teachers College Press.

Dewey, J. (1990). *The school and society. The child and the curriculum.* Chicago: University of Chicago Press. (Original works published 1900, 1902)

Gardner, H. (1983). *Frames of mind.* New York: Basic Books.

Noddings, N. (1994). Does everybody count? Reflections on reforms in school mathematics. *Journal of Mathematical Behavior, 13*(1), 89–104.

SUGGESTED READINGS

Cuban, L. (2008). *Frogs into princes: Writings on school reform.* New York: Teachers College Press.

Glass, H. T. (2006). *Curriculum mapping: A step-by-step guide for creating curriculum year overviews.* Thousand Oaks, CA: Corwin.

Hale, J. A. (Ed.). (2007). *A guide to curriculum mapping: Planning, implementing, and sustaining the process.* Thousand Oaks, CA: Corwin.

Jacobs, H. H. (1997). *Mapping the big picture: Integrating curriculum and assessment K–12.* Alexandria, VA: Association for Supervision and Curriculum Development.

Jacobs, H. H. (Ed.). (2004). *Getting results with curriculum mapping.* Alexandria, VA: Association for Supervision and Curriculum Development.

Kallick, B., & Colosimo, J. (2008). *Using curriculum mapping and assessment data to improve learning.* Thousand Oaks, CA: Corwin.

Lambros, A. (2004). *Problem-based learning in middle and high school classrooms: A teacher's guide to implementation.* Thousand Oaks, CA: Corwin.

Littky, D. (with Grabelle, S.). (2004). *The big picture: Education is everyone's business.* Alexandria, VA: Association for Supervision and Curriculum Development.

Markham, T., Larmer, J., & Ravitz, J. (2003). *Handbook of project-based learning* (2nd ed.). Novato, CA: Buck Institute for Education.

Sehr, D. T. (1997). *Education for public democracy.* Albany: State University of New York Press.

Udelhofen, S. (2005). *Keys to curriculum mapping: Strategies and tools to make it work.* Thousand Oaks, CA: Corwin.

Meeting the Individual Needs of Each Student at an Alternative High School

Prereading Focus Points: The following case study examines ways to enhance and restructure the planned/designed curriculum based on data provided by three sources of information—context, content, and students.

Level: High school

Content Area: English-language arts

Setting: Urban

Spotlight on . . . Enhancement and restructuring of planned/designed curriculum

Key Terms: Inner-ring suburbs; "school within school"; curriculum alignment

BACKGROUND INFORMATION ABOUT THE TEACHER

Sharee is a veteran English-language arts teacher who actively incorporates English-language arts content standards, graduation test preparation, and individualization of instruction into her regular classroom practice. She has worked at the school for 5 years and worked within the district for 5 years before that. Sharee is very familiar with the curriculum and incorporates African American literature and themes as the main component of her instruction. She serves as the literacy lead teacher, a key position in the school's reform efforts. In her position, Sharee takes initiative with regard to the content literacy component by providing professional development and materials to the teachers within her school. She also offers professional development to her peers in the area of content literacy and earnestly wants to provide her own students with the best opportunities for academic success regardless of where they will be doing the work.

Demographers refer to suburbs that are adjacent to central cities as inner-ring (vs. outer-ring and exurbs). **Inner-ring suburbs** often have similar demographics to those of the central city.

Sharee works at Urban High School in a small, "inner-ring" suburb. The school district is struggling to address the needs of its minority community. The district is 99.2% African American and 0.5% multiracial, and it is officially 99.8% economically disadvantaged. The district has recently created four small learning communities (SLCs) as part of the school improvement effort. One SLC is labeled an alternative high school. This "school within school" or "alternative learning program" has approximately 275 students. The alternative aspects of the program address the needs of students who are not able to succeed or cope with the traditional school environment. Some students elect the alternative program, while others are assigned due to their high risk for dropping out. They may also have a history of involvement with the courts and may have been incarcerated. Reasons for incarceration may include drug charges, assault, robbery, and so forth. Teen pregnancy is also a concern in this community. There are a number of students at the school who are parents already. Female students who give birth may take a maternity leave from school.

School within school represents an example of school transformation or restructuring stemming from the principle that a smaller school promotes more positive interactions, leading to better student performance and overall school climate.

Students who are out of school for an extended time due to illness, leave, or incarceration are provided with independent study packets to keep current with their schoolwork. Students receive this work through their classroom teachers. The school works closely with the families and with the juvenile legal system to provide support to students. The students are supposed to complete their work packets and turn them in when they return or through an individual who serves as a courier between the school and the student. The frequency of these structured absence situations is such that it is beneficial to have these materials prepared.

BACKGROUND INFORMATION ABOUT THE CURRICULUM

Specifically, Sharee's small school is reviewing the individualized packets prepared for students who cannot attend school due to a structured absence situation. The current individualized curriculum draws directly from the classroom curriculum. In class, students read a series of novels, most of which were written by African American authors and/or focus on urban themes and issues. They follow the basic curriculum guide laid out by the district and incorporate both the state academic content standards and the requirements for the state graduation test. The curricular materials are structured around a literature core reading series by a large publishing house. Novels are selected from a list provided by the teacher. The reading level is appropriate for ninth-grade students who are reading at or near their grade level.

Sharee works to incorporate the sociocultural perspective on learning into her curricular packets. She incorporates many aspects of the African American cultural experience and also guides the students in classroom activities and in discussions around such themes. Students are provided with opportunities for choice in both activities and assessments. Although, in the classroom, Sharee focuses on an individual learning approach (Dewey, 1902/1990), the independent learning packets require breaking up the material into subunits and step-by-step sequential processes. Using academic content standards as an alignment tool as well as a foundation for the learning objectives in the independent learning packets allows students to create a framework for their learning and to scaffold with prior knowledge whenever possible. The independent aspect to the learning packets requires that the learning be structured in a way that promotes student autonomy while providing adequate support to the learner.

Students who miss school in a structured absence situation are provided with a packet of work material consisting of worksheets, short-answer essays, and copies of the reading material (novel, short story, or passage). Additionally, there is state graduation preparation material comprising questions from previous test materials, questions about the novel, and/or questions about the more general aspects of the graduation test. All these documents are a standard packet for all students who will be missing school for an extended period. Thus, these students are able to keep current with their schoolwork. The material is sequenced into individual units that can be worked on separately.

> **Curriculum alignment** is a complex process by which content standards correlate with subject matter content, instructional strategies and materials, learning opportunities, assessment tools, and evidence of student learning, thus leading to improved student performance.

PROBLEM

First, the curriculum packet consists of standard materials. While it is designed to meet the needs of students who are not able to physically attend school, it is not sufficiently customized to address individual learning needs. Second, the written nature of the packet means that it is most accessible to students who are good readers. However, for those students who are weak or struggling readers the whole process becomes more challenging or even impossible. Unfortunately, the student population that these materials are created for is also likely to be made up of weak or struggling readers. At the very least, these students are likely to be low in their academic engagement and motivation.

Another concern is that in the regular curriculum, the teacher prepares and presents materials as a sequential lesson, but the packet materials are presented as an independent and often discontinuous unit. Additionally, students using these materials are expected to do so independently in an environment that may not be conducive to learning. The visual appeal and approachability of the documents are essential to engaging students who are not in an environment that will necessarily promote or support engagement.

Another issue relates to student motivation, particularly that of students who are not in school for an extended period of time. As motivation is built through relationships between students and teachers as well as through making the work approachable, meaningful, and accessible, the use of independent learning packets requires the use of appropriate incentives for students.

Finally, it is both time- and labor-intensive for teachers to create packets each time there is a need. It would be more efficient if a standardized format could be established and used consistently.

PROBING QUESTIONS

1. How might objectives of the independent learning packets be designed in ways that adequately address student needs and support learning preferences and motivation?

2. How might support to struggling readers be provided as they attempt to access the contents of the independent learning packets?

3. What are some appropriate means by which students could assess their own progress?

PROPOSED SOLUTION

Sharee's proposed solution focuses on enhancing and retooling the independent learning packet materials. The small school is increasing the use of content literacy strategies in all of its curricula. Consequently, the individual learning packets would incorporate content literacy strategies. The plan is to use consistent strategies across content areas in the classroom as a way to allow students to anticipate the process of the unit. This consistency of tools will also be incorporated into the independent study packets.

The proposed curriculum will also incorporate step-by-step incremental instructions. Each unit will have the same basic structure, clear expectations, and a guide to allow students to self-assess their written work. The following steps are being proposed:

a) Clearly articulate the objectives of the independent learning packets.

b) Align ninth-grade English-language arts standards with the planned/designed curriculum and the state graduation test requirements. Build in any missing or correct any deficient areas of the curriculum.

c) Identify individual units based on the revised curriculum.

d) Identify and select visual support systems by using graphic organizers as an integral part of the curriculum. Create written instructions for each graphic organizer. Instructions need to be general enough that they will apply equally well to a variety of units, thus leading to consistency across units within the curriculum. Students will become familiar with the format of using one of the graphic organizers within the unit, and then they will be able to predict the application. Student choices should be incorporated at this point.

e) Ensure access to reading materials. Review them to determine the reading level and if any necessary supporting materials and instructions are needed. Select parallel materials that will permit multiple levels that address the same academic content standards. Put together a file of electronic materials that can be printed as needed at various levels. This would take into account the different reading proficiency levels students might demonstrate prior to the self-paced instructional sequence.

f) Write clear, sequential instructions that allow a student to proceed through each unit independently.

g) Create self-assessment tools that can be used independently by each student. These tools would also have to relate to the prior knowledge and skills individual students may have as they progress through the independent learning packets. Thus, they would become aware of their own needs as they emerge in the learning process.

h) Create writing outcomes and instructions. Also, develop writing rubrics that can be used to self-assess any written items.

i) Design a notebook and/or an electronic file that contains instructions, the required reading materials and alternates, and the graphic organizers to allow the teacher to assemble quickly the materials based on the length of time that students will be absent.

EXPECTED OUTCOMES

By implementing the solutions proposed above, Sharee expects the following at her school:

1. A clearer, more cohesive collection of curricular materials will be designed specifically for independent study use.

2. All curricular units will be aligned both with corresponding English-language arts content standards and with state graduation test requirements. Clear learning objectives will be identified for each student.

3. All curricular units will contain materials that allow students to work at their individual reading level while still addressing their content learning.

4. A selection of appropriate tasks and corresponding graphic organizers will make use of student choice as a means to increase both engagement and interest.

5. Clear, sequential instructions will allow students to work independently but with full understanding of the process and bolts of the unit.

6. Self-assessment rubrics will provide students with a framework for reviewing and monitoring their own work.

POINTS TO PONDER . . .

Sharee has done a commendable job of identifying concerns in her classroom and school, and she has shown a great ability to reflect and problem-solve. She lists many steps to resolve her concerns. What could become a challenge at any of these steps? Do you believe that students should be identified, pulled out, and placed into such schools? What integrative/inclusive alternative would you have to this type of "alternative" high school?

QUESTIONS FOR ADMINISTRATORS

As the principal of this small school, what implementation problems do you foresee with Sharee's recommended plan of action? What kind of support would you have to offer her plan in order to succeed? How would you involve the community in successfully implementing the revised independent learning packets? Would your involvement in the process be any different if you were the superintendent?

IN-CLASS ACTIVITY

In a group of four or five members representing a variety of grade levels and content areas, discuss the pros and cons of the implementation of "individual education plans" for all students. That is, assuming that all students are unique in their needs, desires, and abilities, how can you ensure that the schooling process meets all of these? More important, how would such "individual education plans" impact the curriculum management process at the district level? Have a recorder take notes onto chart paper and a reporter briefly explain these notes to the whole class.

REFERENCE

Dewey, J. (1990). *The school and society. The child and the curriculum.* Chicago: University of Chicago Press. (Original works published 1900, 1902)

SUGGESTED READINGS

Cotton, K. (1996). *School size, school climate, and student performance: Close-up #20.* Portland, OR: Northwest Regional Educational Laboratory.

Dewey, J. (1997). *Experience and education.* New York: Touchstone. (Original work published 1938)

Littky, D., & Grabelle, S. (2004). *The big picture: Education is everyone's business.* Alexandria, VA: Association for Supervision and Curriculum Development.

Squires, D. A. (2005). *Aligning and balancing the standards-based curriculum.* Thousand Oaks, CA: Corwin.

Squires, D. A. (2009). *Curriculum alignment: Research-based strategies for increasing student achievement.* Thousand Oaks, CA: Corwin.

CASE 4

Using Assessment and Student Interest Data to Inform Differentiated Instruction in an Inclusive Classroom

Prereading Focus Points: A middle school teacher attempts to bridge the gap between her students' mathematical aptitudes and instruction based on the State Academic Content Standards representing her district's planned/designed curriculum. The author takes into account the preassessment of students' content area knowledge and skills as well as the differentiated instruction to meet the needs of all students in her inclusive classroom. Data-driven instructional decision making and curriculum mapping support her efforts.

Level: Middle school

Content Area: Math

Setting: Urban

Spotlight on . . .

a) Accurately quantifying students' content area knowledge and skills in an attempt to increase standardized test scores;

b) Identifying and providing support and resources to meet the needs of students of varying abilities based on enhanced awareness of their background.

Key Terms: Invisible culture; standards-driven curriculum; Saxon Math; Continuous Improvement Plan; short-cycle assessment

BACKGROUND INFORMATION ABOUT THE TEACHER AND THE CONTEXT

Marlena is a fourth-grade teacher in an urban setting—a large Midwestern city that is very diverse and whose students face the typical range of problems of 21st-century inner-city schools. For 6 years she has been working with sixth-grade gifted students in math and science. The sixth-grade class is a self-contained gifted unit. This year she opted to move to a fourth-grade regular education classroom with a cluster group of gifted students (4 students in the formal program) and students with Written Education Plans (WEPs) in specific areas for a total of 11 students identified with areas of giftedness. The class also contains 4 students with a 504 plan who have been diagnosed with attention deficit hyperactivity disorder, in addition to 3 students who have Individualized Education Plans (IEPs)—1 for other health impairment (OHI), who has an aide assigned to him, and 2 others who have a learning disability. The school practices total inclusion. Therefore, students with IEPs are not pulled out for individual instruction. Instead, the specialist comes to their class to coteach the lessons and make the necessary modifications. The students in the formal gifted program are pulled out of class for 3 hours each week for small-group instruction.

The students have a broad range of abilities when it comes to mathematical aptitude. The continuum ranges from problems with basic single-digit addition to being able to solve multiple-step problems, decipher order of operations, and solve algebraic equations.

Marlena believes that teachers should tap into what students know and are able to do as a starting point in their professional responsibilities in the classroom. Additionally, teachers should be aware of the social conditions of their students and how the school environment promotes their abilities. This further indicates that teachers must be cognizant of the invisible culture of their students. Marlena feels she must understand the nuances and subtleties of a child's culture, background, and upbringing to fully understand the child and to see what the child holds valuable. Moreover, she sees the school as a community that engages parents as an integral part of that community. With this in mind, Marlena believes that the curriculum must be explained to parents in order to be effectively implemented in the classroom.

> **Invisible culture** is the sum of all aspects of one's cultural characteristics not available to conscious awareness.

BACKGROUND INFORMATION ABOUT THE CURRICULUM

Marlena is currently using the State Academic Content Standards (SACS) as a basis for the identification of instructional objectives. The State Department of Education (SDE) states in the SACS for mathematics that every student should have access to a standards-driven curriculum that challenges and promotes learning. The SDE further states that curricula need to be adjusted based on the full range of student needs, from learning disabilities to giftedness and talent.

The SACS also stipulate that mathematics should be taught by making real-world connections. Teachers should develop lessons and assessments that are considered relevant to students. The SACS focus on the fact that learners must be engaged in real-life experiences. Whether content is to be introduced before context or whether context is to be addressed before content is all at the discretion of teachers. While the SDE attempts to make this appear child-centered, the reality is different. If one looks at the Writing Team for the Mathematics Standards, one will notice that the team comprises business leaders, teachers, and a few parents. Students and child development specialists are noticeably absent. Society is dictating what the child will learn and when. This makes one wonder about the driving force behind this type of curriculum—the knowledge and skills necessary to pursue efficiency upon graduation and joining of the workforce.

> Recent school reform efforts mention **standards-driven curriculum** as an example of integrating content standards into teaching, learning, and assessment.

The school board has adopted the SDE's Academic Content Standards as the main curriculum for the district. It has also adopted the Saxon Math series as the planned/designed curriculum. The principal of the school has stated that Saxon materials must be used in daily lesson plans. It should be noted that the school has a curriculum review committee meant to explore the relationship between the Saxon Math series and the SACS. The committee's recommendation, approved by the school board, emphasized a timeline for the implementation of the Saxon lessons. Therefore, the committee created a document called the Math Task Force Advisory, which details the base timeline as well as the supplemental materials needed, in addition to specifying when to implement the supplementary information.

> **Saxon Math** is a K–12 program that relies on a gradual approach to the introduction of new mathematical concepts and skills.

The Continuous Improvement Plan (CIP) for the school has stipulated the goal for fourth grade is to have 75% of the students pass the State Mathematics Achievement Test. The baseline data are taken from the State Fourth-Grade Proficiency Test results from the previous year—the passage rate for the fourth graders was 46%. The district is in a financial crisis, as are many other districts. Taxpayers, as stakeholders, are looking at test scores to deem if their money is being spent wisely on schools. They want to know what schools are doing to increase test scores. Because of the information presented in the local and national media, many feel that standardized test scores are the only effective measure to see if children are learning. The school's Building Management Team is hearing this pressure and creating the CIP accordingly.

> **Continuous Improvement Plan (CIP)** represents a document that connects the mission and vision statements, as well as specific benchmarks and indicators, at the district level with strengths, areas of improvement, actions, expected outcomes, and a timeline at the school level.

PROBLEM

Marlena is obviously faced with a very diverse student population and a building management team driven by a clear task to improve test scores. She has several gifted children not being taught at a level appropriately paced for them, which means that their special needs are not being adequately met. The students identified as gifted in the area of mathematics have scored in the 95th percentile on the California Achievement Test (CAT). There is a high probability that these students will pass the fourth-grade achievement test based on the previous test scores. At the same time, the students with learning disabilities scored significantly lower on the CAT. The problem with these types of tests is that they do not specifically show a child's strengths and weaknesses according to the benchmarks. While the IEPs adequately specify the students' needs, they are not aligned with the SACS for mathematics at the grade level. Oftentimes, these IEPs require time out of the regular class and into the resource room. The school's policy for special education is full inclusion where the special education specialist comes into the room to help teach the lesson.

The complaints heard often in class and at parent–teacher conferences are as follows:

1. My child has an IEP and is required to be in the resource room, so why is he/she being taught in the regular education room?

2. My child is bored. My child is a math genius. What are you going to do for my child so he/she is not bored?

3. My child is lost. The homework is too hard. Where can I get a tutor? Can my child have a learning disability? When can you test my child?

4. What is going to be on the achievement test? What are you doing to get my child ready for the achievement test?

5. What math program are you using? Is it in line with the SACS?

PROBING QUESTIONS

1. How could the mathematical knowledge and skills of each student be determined accurately?

2. How could individual instruction for enrichment and remediation be provided?

3. How could areas of additional assistance be identified before the achievement test is administered?

PROPOSED SOLUTION

Because SACS and achievement testing are a fundamental component of today's curriculum, any solution needs to explore the full engagement of learners based on their academic readiness. In this light, the proposed solution would involve the following steps:

1. Determine the proficiency level for each fourth-grade student at the beginning of the year by taking into account the corresponding benchmarks— number sense, measurement, geometry, functions and algebra, patterns, data analysis, and mathematical process. This can be accomplished by administering a pretest to be followed up with a posttest. In this case, the achievement test could be used as a posttest. In an attempt to monitor all fourth graders in the school, the math department will write a pretest that combines five (or more) questions geared toward identifying strengths and weaknesses in each benchmark. It would be a good idea to write a grant proposal so that the teachers are compensated for their time needed to write quality pretests and short-cycle assessments.

2. Using these data, individual teachers can then work with flexible groups. For example, those students who have mastered the geometry pretest will be grouped together for enrichment opportunities, and those who need additional help will be grouped together for remediation. This flexible grouping arrangement allows those students to work together on a project that is standards-based but is at a level that is appropriate and comfortable for them, whether they are gifted or learning disabled.

3. The teacher would also utilize short-cycle assessments throughout the year to ensure the students are learning along the way. These short-cycle assessments will be written by individual teachers or collaboratively by the whole math department.

This hopefully will prevent students from falling through the cracks by providing them with the necessary additional assistance, remediation, and diagnostic work. At the same time, it will provide enrichment opportunities for those students who have mastered the concept. All this will be done to ensure that all students show growth and progress. The pretests and short-cycle tests will document that children are making annual yearly progress. This information could be presented to the Building Management Team to show progress and to help refine the school's CIP.

4. The special education teacher assigned to the class would be working with small groups—not only for those students who have special needs but also

for those students who are having trouble with a specific concept or skill specified by any given benchmark. By doing this, they could determine whether or not a student should be tested for a learning disability. The gifted intervention specialist would also be utilized to provide special activities to develop the talents and abilities of the students who have been identified as gifted. The regular education teacher would then be working with the rest of the class to make sure the content is mastered. The special education teacher, along with the Intervention Assistance Team, will rewrite the IEPs to make sure that students are included in the regular education class and are not pulled out to the resource room unless there is clear evidence that the latter is the least restrictive environment for a particular child.

Individual teachers as well as the whole math department will use the district's Math Task Force document as an aid in instruction to make sure the Saxon Math series adequately prepares students for the short-cycle assessment as well as for the achievement test. Additionally, the classroom teacher will design and implement a student interest survey to gather information about the students' background in order to understand their culture (both visible and invisible) and to gain insight into their learning styles. This information will be utilized when planning learning experiences for them in a way that is tailored to their needs. If children are engaged and feel a personal connection to the information presented, they will feel that they have a say in what is being taught and thus become more actively involved in the educational process. Because a child's interests and needs change throughout the year, the survey needs to be updated each grading period. This information could be used to map out the curriculum for the school year.

EXPECTED OUTCOMES

This plan is intended to allow for flexible grouping and for individualized instruction. It would also encourage teachers to document their students' specific strengths and weaknesses related to the expected content area proficiency. At the same time, teachers would be able to show parents evidence related to where their child is in terms of growth and progress in the area of mathematics. The special education specialist would be a more integral part of the class as he or she would be working with a variety of children, not just the ones with IEPs. The gifted intervention specialist would also be provided the opportunity to work with children other than the ones in the formal program.

It should be noted that this plan calls for little or no money. The initial investment of time to produce quality pretests and short-cycle assessments could be a stumbling block for some, and that is where a grant opportunity comes into play. Even if a grant is not an option, individual teachers, students, and the whole school would have much to gain from implementing this plan.

Marlena will be better equipped to answer the many questions raised by parents and community members because she will have data to support her choices for curriculum implementation. It is ultimately the teacher's prerogative to determine the scope of the taught curriculum based on the planned/designed curriculum. By identifying students' strengths and weaknesses, the teacher could focus on involving students in the selection of projects geared toward enhancing strengths and correcting deficiencies. Once a teacher understands where each child is academically and socially, objectives can be selected and learning experiences can be tailored to the interests of the child. Time spent on sequencing and organizing the learning experiences can be maximized. Lastly, assessments—both summative and formative—could be administered throughout the year and will provide a clearer vision of what the child has learned and mastered.

> **Short-cycle assessments** are formative in nature; they do not take a lot of time to implement, thus providing teachers with data related to the progress of their students.

POINTS TO PONDER . . .

What steps would you recommend to any curriculum team (at a level of your choice) in its attempt to analyze how the planned/designed curriculum aligns with preset content standards while accommodating the full range of student needs through differentiation? What would be a useful template that could be implemented as support for the analysis? Within this template, what should be the starting point? How should work progress? What would be an endpoint that indicates the opportunity for piloting a plan of action based on the findings of the analysis process?

QUESTIONS FOR ADMINISTRATORS

Given the prominence of accountability requirements in today's field of education, what are some of the specific actions you would take to involve your school community in the analysis of assessment data (standardized as well as alternative/authentic) based on which an enrichment curriculum might be strengthened? The same question could be asked when dealing with remedial instruction. What means of communication would you use as school principal to maintain the momentum of such curriculum revisioning work?

IN-CLASS ACTIVITY

In groups of four to five members (representing different content areas or specializations), draft the outline of a daylong professional development opportunity on differentiated instruction for both special education and regular education teachers in a district that you are familiar with. As an alternative, your group could focus on alternative means of assessment to be used in inclusive classrooms.

To identify the specifics of the student body in your chosen school district, you may have to access relevant Web-based resources in preparation for this activity.

As a group, prepare an oral presentation of the highlights of the professional development activity in question—start, main content, and end—paying attention to assessment and evaluation of the whole activity. You may also want to generate some ideas about the creation of a repository of materials and resources that participants would have access to at the conclusion of the professional development opportunity.

SUGGESTED READINGS

Banks, J. A., & Banks, C. A. M. (Eds.). (2004). *Multicultural education: Issues and perspectives* (5th ed.). Hoboken, NJ: Wiley.

Butler, S. M., & McMunn, N. D. (2006). *A teacher's guide to classroom assessment: Understanding and using assessment to improve student learning.* San Francisco: Jossey-Bass.

Glatthorn, A. A., Boschee, F., & Whitehead, B. M. (2009). *Curriculum leadership: Strategies for development and implementation* (2nd ed.). Thousand Oaks, CA: Sage.

Grant, C. A., & Sleeter, C. E. (2007). *Doing multicultural education for achievement and equity.* New York: Routledge.

Lang, S., Stanley, T., & Moore, B. (2008). *Short cycle assessment: Improving student achievement through formative assessment.* Larchmont, NY: Eye on Education.

Popham, W. J. (2008). *Transformative assessment.* Alexandria, VA: Association for Supervision and Curriculum Development.

CASE 5

Motivating Students to Learn in a Peer-Supported School Environment

Prereading Focus Points: A private school teacher at the kindergarten level notices that in spite of her school's commitment to the basic principles of differentiated instruction, there is no formal procedure to determine how that is implemented by teachers. The fact that school administration recommends the use of peer observations and constructive criticism does not seem to help the teacher come up with ideas to motivate students and sustain their learning.

Level: Kindergarten

Content Area: English-language arts (reading)

Setting: Urban

Spotlight on . . .

    a) Student choices in learning; and
    b) Sustainable student engagement in learning activities.

Key Terms: Performance objectives; outcomes-based curriculum; connoisseurship model; Universal Design for Learning

BACKGROUND INFORMATION ABOUT THE TEACHER

Amber teaches at a private school with an urban focus. There are approximately 440 students who attend the school, which serves students from preschool to eighth grade. The school is nongraded and affiliated with a Catholic diocese in the area. Students are grouped in multiage classrooms referred to as levels as opposed to the traditional grades system. The school's mission emphasizes the provision of a quality, individualized, Catholic/Christian education to children living in the area, particularly to those who, otherwise, might not have access to education at all.

Amber is in her third year of teaching at the kindergarten level. She has an early childhood education degree and an intervention specialist degree, both from a private college in the area. Amber is currently working toward a master's degree in education with a concentration in educational technology.

Her classroom consists of 16 5- and 6-year-olds coming from varied backgrounds, though most of them are from single-parent, lower-income families. These students have varied abilities. They attended day care or a Head Start program before enrolling at the school. These children are under Amber's supervision from 8:00 a.m. to 3:00 p.m. Monday through Friday. They are allotted 20 minutes for lunch and 20 minutes for recess daily. They work on reading, math, writing, science, social skills, and religion every day.

BACKGROUND INFORMATION ABOUT THE CURRICULUM

The school's curriculum is strongly based on the philosophy of Catholic education. The written curriculum for each content area begins with several goals related to Catholic education. For instance, one of the English-language arts curriculum goals is *to communicate the gospel message of Jesus.* One of the objectives under oral communication for the kindergarten curriculum states that "learners will demonstrate the ability to share orally information and experiences." This objective then directly relates to the goal of communicating the gospel. Every goal is followed by its corresponding instructional objectives, as in the example above. They are meant to be statements of what we expect students to demonstrate as a result of having engaged in appropriate learning activities. Performance objectives are also mentioned, as they are observable indicators of student learning. Finally, assessment strategies and tools are stated.

> **Performance objectives** state the expected level of student performance or proficiency as a result of engaging in an instructional activity designed to help students meet the set objective.

The course of study for each content area creates a framework of continuous progress from kindergarten to the eighth level. Teachers use the curriculum's sequential learning objectives as a guide to meet individual needs of learners. The objectives represent benchmarks that give teachers an expected level of competency for the average student. This curriculum is performance-driven and outcomes-based. Consequently, the school has developed standardized procedures and assessments listed in the course of study for critical areas

> **Outcomes-based curriculum** places the identification of instructional outcomes as the basis for any planning efforts, thus leading to student performance supposed to evidence the same outcomes.

of the curriculum. This helps ensure a correspondence between the written, implemented, and assessed curriculum.

The school's philosophy is based on the differentiation principles noted by Carol Ann Tomlinson, multiage classrooms, and nongraded assessments. Each teacher is required to use the basic differentiation principles of meeting student needs, beginning where the learner is, varying grouping formats, and using a variety of assessment techniques when implementing the planned curriculum.

Each new teacher is given a large binder that contains the school's written curriculum. Teachers are encouraged to enact the curriculum using differentiation principles, although there is no formal procedure to check how they actually implement the designed curriculum. Amber tries to engage her students in learning experiences through fun, interactive activities based on their readiness levels and learning style preferences.

Amber's school follows Eisner's educational connoisseurship model. In this light, students do not receive letter grades, meaning that authentic forms of assessment are essential. All children begin to work on a portfolio in kindergarten by selecting writing samples, religious prayers, projects, and artwork to be included. Each piece selected by students for inclusion in the portfolio must be accompanied by a written reflection. Students continue to add to their portfolio until their graduation from the eighth level.

> Eisner's (1979) **connoisseurship model** relies on empirical evidence leading to appreciation of what is significant in educational settings.

The school principal also requires all teachers to visit other classrooms in the building. While visiting, they are asked to take notes about pedagogical methods and ideas that they could adapt in implementing the written curriculum in their own classrooms. At the end of the clinical observation session, teachers are encouraged to write up a report about the reflection on the experience, as well as provide constructive criticism to the classroom teacher observed. This process is very similar to Eisner's procedure where professional evaluators offer suggestions for improvement.

In order to differentiate instruction, Amber groups her students in reading and math based on their ability. Currently she has three reading groups and two math groups that are very fluid and can change monthly based on student achievement and progress. Each group works at its own pace and is engaged in curriculum at its ability level.

PROBLEM

Five of Amber's students are unmotivated and usually are not fully engaged in the activities or assignments they are given during seatwork time. Completing and turning in seatwork during reading instruction seems to be their biggest challenge. During a typical 70-minute reading block, students rotate between reading centers. For approximately 20 minutes they work directly with the teacher, followed first by 20 minutes of student work assisted by an instructional aide and next by 20 minutes of seatwork providing students with an opportunity to complete a worksheet or project based on a skill they have been learning.

Through her direct observations, Amber noticed these particular students resting their heads on the table and looking out the window. When reviewing papers completed for the day, she also realized that these students usually do not turn in the assignments. She concluded that her students lack motivation and need encouragement to stay engaged while working without the teacher's close presence by their seats.

Over the course of the past trimester Amber tried unsuccessfully to use verbal praise and modeling to encourage these students. It seemed to work for two of the students but only for a short period of time. Therefore, it is increasingly difficult for her to stop working with a small group in order to constantly remind particular students to stay focused and complete their assignments.

PROBING QUESTIONS

1. How could Amber give her students choices when working at their seats while having them practice/meet the learning objectives set for them?

2. What strategies could Amber use to motivate students and sustain their learning over the course of a whole lesson?

PROPOSED SOLUTION

The Universal Design for Learning, utilized by hundreds of teachers to meet individual needs of their students, has three basic principles:

Universal Design for Learning (UDL) is a framework that relies on a balance between high standards and student diversity in ways that maximize individual learning.

1. Representation—there are multiple ways teachers can present information.
2. Expression—there are multiple ways students can express or show what they have learned.
3. Engagement—there are multiple methods to engage and motivate students.

The last principle is the one that Amber could focus on while employing the following three new methods:

1. Choice of tools—typically students in her class are permitted to use yellow, Laddie pencils. She could begin to allow students to select a writing utensil of their choice. With this in mind, Amber could put regular Laddie pencils, colored pencils, and pencils with different designs on them in a large cup on the writing table. Students will be encouraged to select a writing utensil at the beginning of the seatwork to use on their assignments.

2. Choice of rewards—currently students are not rewarded when they complete an assignment. Instead, they are usually punished (i.e., miss part of workstations to finish their work) when they fail to turn in an assignment. Amber could begin to reward students who pace themselves appropriately and complete their work within the allotted 20 minutes with extra, fun activities. For instance, if a student completes his or her assignment in 10 minutes, then he or she can choose an extra activity as a reward. These activities could include computer time, listening to a book at the listening center, or playing with play dough.

3. Choice of context—presently students are asked to work independently and only request "buddy" assistance if they need help. Amber could begin to allow students to choose whom to work with as a way to spark interest in collaborative efforts.

Even though not all her students have motivation issues, Amber could enact these changes with all 16 of her students, as they are easy to implement and do not require weeks of practicing new routines. She should explain these new changes each day for one week during their daily Morning Meeting, where she could model how to select a pencil, choose an extra activity, and/or select a partner to work with. After one week, Amber could assist students on an individual basis, whenever the new choices may cause confusion.

EXPECTED OUTCOMES

Amber hopes that by making these changes in the way the student engagement is structured in her classroom, students will become motivated to complete their daily seatwork assignments. She also hopes they will begin to put more effort into their work and turn in "polished" assignments. Finally, these changes could sustain student learning, leading to a greater chance of mastering the curriculum goals.

By providing students with a choice of tools, students will really be motivated to begin working on the assignments. Children of 5 and 6 years are very drawn to anything new and flashy. As far as the choice of rewards is concerned, it may motivate students to complete and turn in the assignments because they will be eager to choose a fun activity afterward. Finally, the choice of context will help students struggling to complete the task because of boredom or inability to comprehend the task at hand. Allowing them the choice of a partner to work with will provide the peer support needed. Students at this age are very social and like to work with their friends to accomplish an activity.

POINTS TO PONDER . . .

Amber's fellow teachers use peer observation and review to provide each other with constructive criticism aimed at improving classroom practice. Considering the "framework of continuous progress from kindergarten to the eighth level" in place at her school, how would you use the elements of Eisner's "connoisseurship model" of curriculum evaluation to make appropriate recommendations pertaining to motivating students? How would you use the peer support system to identify and communicate effective motivating strategies as part of the Universal Design for Learning paradigm?

QUESTIONS FOR ADMINISTRATORS

Put yourselves in the shoes of Amber's school principal, a fervent proponent of peer observation and review. How would you balance the "micro" level of what seems to be significant at the classroom level (such as Amber's student motivation issue) and the macro level of supporting the "connoisseurship" model for the whole school? What would you do to inform schoolwide decisions that promote differentiation in the various classrooms? In turn, how would you be able to resort to evidence of effective differentiation to "keep the whole school running well"?

Form groups that should, ideally, have at least one English-language arts specialist. As a group, brainstorm ideas and come up with suggestions for Amber on how she might be able to use "student mentorship" (Glatthorn, Boschee, & Whitehead, 2009, p. 341) as a way to differentiate the reading curriculum. Prepare a group presentation for the rest of the class, based on which you could formulate a formal "plan of action" that Amber could implement in her classroom/school.

REFERENCES

Center for Applied Special Technology. (2008). *Universal design for learning guidelines version 1.0.* Wakefield, MA: Author.

Eisner, E. W. (1979). *The educational imagination.* Upper Saddle River, NJ: Merrill/Prentice Hall.

Glatthorn, A. A., Boschee, F., & Whitehead, B. M. (2009). *Curriculum leadership: Strategies for development and implementation* (2nd ed.). Thousand Oaks, CA: Sage.

SUGGESTED READINGS

Fried, R. L. (2001). *The passionate teacher: A practical guide.* Boston: Beacon Press.

Fried, R. L. (2002). *The passionate student: How teachers and parents can help children reclaim the joy of discovery.* Boston: Beacon Press.

Henson, K. T. (2001). *Curriculum planning: Integrating multiculturalism, constructivism, and education reform* (2nd ed.). Long Grove, IL: Waveland Press, Inc.

Tomlinson, C. A. (2003). *Fulfilling the promise of the differentiated classroom: Strategies and tools for responsive teaching.* Alexandria, VA: Association for Supervision and Curriculum Development.

Authentic Audience and Affective Learning in a Gifted and Talented Middle School Program

Prereading Focus Points: Content integration for a teacher of gifted and talented middle school students is made possible by engaging in careful interdisciplinary planning. Sparking learners' interest can be sustained by tapping into their affective domain when creating learning opportunities whose outcomes are "authentic audiences."

Level: Middle school

Content Area: All core subjects

Setting: Suburban

Spotlight on . . .

a) Gifted and talented learners;
b) Affective learning;
c) Teachable moments;
d) Authentic learning; and
e) Content integration.

Key Terms: Highly Qualified Teacher; affective learning; Parallel Curriculum Model; Enrichment Triad

BACKGROUND INFORMATION ABOUT THE TEACHER

Corinne has been teaching for 7 years in a variety of settings. She taught gifted and talented students in the third through fifth grades in a pull-out model; fifth grade in a regular, self-contained classroom; and seventh- and

"Highly Qualified Teacher" (HQT) represents the designation classroom practitioners receive based on specific criteria outlined by the No Child Left Behind Act.

eighth-grade language arts in a middle school. She received her license in gifted education in 1997 and has been in her current position for 1 year. Corinne currently teaches a fifth-grade, gifted and talented, self-contained class. The gifted and talented program is housed in one elementary school in a suburban school district. The students qualifying for the program are transported from their home schools to Ayres Elementary where the program is located. Ayres Elementary has an enrollment of 600 students in grades K–6. The student body is 84% White, 9% Asian, and 7% other. Of all students, 8.1% are considered disadvantaged, while 6.1% are identified with disabilities. There are 27 classroom teachers, 11 special area teachers, and nine aides and small-group instructors. All of the certified teachers are "Highly Qualified," according to state designation. There is one gifted and talented classroom for each grade, second to sixth. All teachers in the program have their license in gifted and talented education. The fifth-grade teacher teaches all core subjects including language arts, social studies, math, science, and health.

BACKGROUND INFORMATION ABOUT THE CURRICULUM

The planned curriculum Corinne is currently using relies on the state content standards. The gifted and talented program uses the same content standards as the regular classroom teachers. However, the program accelerates and enriches the given curriculum. For instance, students are accelerated in math. Fifth-grade students are completing sixth-grade math and use a program called Connected Mathematics, which is a Dale Seymour series. The program has adopted a new reading and language arts series called Pegasus by Kendall Hunt. In addition to the series, Corinne uses Junior Great Books and guided reading groups based on the students' reading levels. The social studies series by Scott Foresman has been recently adopted by the school district.

The fifth-grade focus for social studies is the United States. The text begins with an overview of the American people and land. It then moves through American history beginning with Native Americans and ending with World War II. Each unit has a comprehensive planning guide for the teacher, which includes pacing, main ideas, vocabulary, resources, strategies/activities for meeting individual needs, and various types of assessment options. The guide also includes ways to integrate the curriculum, a read-aloud, and a bibliography of suggested titles.

Due to the nature and needs of the students in the gifted and talented program, emphasis is placed on individualization as well as on the content required by state standards. The teacher is able to move at a faster pace and act as a facilitator in the classroom. Students have more choices in terms of product/performance and areas of independent study. There are also opportunities for students to research topics of interest and present their findings to the rest of the class.

In addition to the planned curriculum, Corinne utilizes class time for affective learning, where social skills are targeted on an as-needed basis. Currently, her class requires discussion of getting along with others and accepting differences. The teacher is assisted by the guidance counselor, and many of the students meet with this professional on an individual basis.

> Learning mediated through the affective domain by having students demonstrate a range of emotional intensity as a reaction to stimuli is considered **affective learning**.

PROBLEM

Last November, Kevin, a fifth grader in Corinne's class, brought in a letter from the United Service Organizations (USO) to share with the class. The letter represented a request for items needed by soldiers overseas. Kevin was asking his classmates to bring in any items so that he could deliver them to the local USO office. Consequently, the rest of the class became very excited—hands shot up and conversations began, as students were full of ideas and questions. It did not take long for the whole class to agree on the schoolwide collection for the USO. The class formed groups, each of which presented its project to each classroom in the school. Students made collection boxes and gathered items regularly. They also wrote thank-you letters to the soldiers they were collecting for, and finally, they went to the USO office to pack boxes, organize the goods, place mailing labels on boxes, and stack them for delivery. Overall, students were thrilled with their efforts. When they returned to class, they wrote reflection papers. Many of them commented on the good feeling of helping others. Corinne felt that the experience was very worthwhile. Not only were students learning, but they were also engaged in authentic experiences that gave them a sense of accomplishment. Typically, when using traditional teaching strategies, some students can become bored quickly, which leads to comments such as "Why do we need to know this?" They often have difficulty applying ideas presented in one subject area to another, with obvious implications on the transfer of knowledge and skills to real-life situations. Corinne would like to be able to incorporate more of such authentic learning opportunities into her curriculum.

PROBING QUESTIONS

1. How could Corinne go about integrating content in ways that motivate gifted and talented learners?

2. Where would Corinne find an "authentic audience" for her students to present the outcomes of their learning?

PROPOSED SOLUTION

> The **Parallel Curriculum Model** supports the development of curricula by selecting a range of "parallel" ways in which to select and design content intended to challenge learners.

> The **Enrichment Triad** is a curriculum model in gifted education that features three interrelated types of enrichment activities focused on general exploration, group training, and individual as well as small-group investigations of real-life problems.

Corinne could integrate multiple content areas and embed state standards into thematic units in order to provide the two key components of good curriculum for gifted and advanced learners: challenge and choice. Yet another option would be thematic units based on essential questions and advanced concepts using the Parallel Curriculum Model (Tomlinson et al., 2009) or Renzulli's Enrichment Triad (Renzulli, Gubbins, McMillen, Eckert, & Little, 2009). Effective differentiated curriculum and instruction adjust the content, the process, and the product in order to create learning experiences that meet the unique needs of advanced learners.

Irrespective of the path to follow, planning an integrated unit is very important. Corinne should develop a yearly plan that allows for such cross-disciplinary learning episodes. With this in mind, the plan should take into account particular units or themes that would emphasize integrative skills areas, along with time frames and required instructional resources for each unit or theme. Given the fluid nature of any given school day, Corinne should consider various school events or activities that may impact the implementation of the integrated unit.

For practical reasons, Corinne could use the following planning sequence adapted from Glatthorn (2004):

1. Consider integration: What particular content areas or subareas will be integrated?

2. Block the unit or theme: title, length, goals, and outcomes.

3. Identify the problem to be addressed: What new approach can we develop? How could we achieve this goal?

4. Draft the unit or theme scenarios: Describe the "big picture"—how will the unit begin? How will it end? What are the necessary intermediary stages of learning?

5. Determine prior knowledge and/or skills needed to succeed as well as the appropriate means of access to information: How will students gain the knowledge required to solve the problem supporting the authentic learning experience? What strategies are appropriate to present information?

6. Determine appropriate learning strategies to be used by students: Which learning strategies are new versus familiar to students? What is the best way to model them?

7. Sequence individual lesson plans.

8. Evaluate and disseminate the unit or theme: Measure the degree to which learning outcomes have been met. How has differentiation supported meaningful learning? Have critical thinking and creativity been encouraged?

One example of a unit that Corinne could integrate for her fifth-grade gifted and talented learners focuses on recycling. In this light, the teacher could incorporate standards applicable to science, social studies, and language arts. Students would be asked to identify if there is a need for a recycling program in their elementary school. Following preliminary conclusions, learners would then investigate community resources and study the history of recycling (in terms of both local and regional/national efforts), leading to a series of proposals for a plan of action to be presented publicly to school administrators, teachers, fellow students, and the Parent-Teacher Association (PTA). Upon approval, students would be responsible for carrying out their proposed plans based on a preset project timeline.

EXPECTED OUTCOMES

Some of the outcomes of engaging in this type of integrated curriculum featuring real-life problems are as follows:

- Intrinsic student motivation will increase.
- Students will be more likely to connect school-based learning with applications of their knowledge and skills to life outside of school.

- Teachers can collaborate on identifying appropriate instructional resources and strategies to meet the needs of all students.
- Students have the choice of product to evidence learning, based on which individualization could be implemented.
- Students could use skills that cut across content areas to solve real-life problems.

POINTS TO PONDER . . .

Corinne relates to the affective domain when differentiating the learning of her students. The approaches she proposes for the integration of content areas in her classroom take into account specific components of an inter-disciplinary planning process. While considering general education programs, how would you address any issues typically associated with the gifted and talented "program scope," such as "grouping, selection, and evaluation" (Wiles, 2005, p. 177)? Moreover, how would you use Corinne's experience to develop appropriately accelerated curricula for gifted and talented learners?

QUESTIONS FOR ADMINISTRATORS

As Corinne's principal, what would you look for in a classroom as evidence of appropriate differentiation for gifted and talented students? Focusing on Corinne's situation, how would you support her use of creativity-focused lessons in heterogeneous classrooms that could accommodate the needs of gifted and talented learners? As a background reading, we recommend Mildrum's (2006) *Creativity Workshops in the Regular Classroom*.

IN-CLASS ACTIVITY

In groups of six members, outline interdisciplinary task design prompts following the GRASPS sequence proposed by Wiggins and McTighe (2005): Goal, Role, Audience, Situation, Performance, and Standards. Share with the rest of the class how you would be able to implement such a performance task sequence to assess student understanding.

REFERENCES

Glatthorn, A. A. (2004). *Developing a quality curriculum*. Long Grove, IL: Waveland Press, Inc.

Mildrum, N. K. (2006). Creativity workshops in the regular classroom. In F. W. Parkway, E. J. Anctil, & G. Hass (Eds.), *Curriculum planning: A contemporary approach* (pp. 411–415). Boston: Allyn & Bacon.

Wiggins, G., & McTighe, J. (2005). *Understanding by design* (2nd ed.). Upper Saddle River, NJ: Pearson.

Wiles, J. (2005). *Curriculum essentials: A resource for educators* (2nd ed.). Boston: Allyn & Bacon.

SUGGESTED READINGS

Betts, G. T., & Kercher, J. K. (1999). *The autonomous learner model: Optimizing ability*. Greeley, CO: ALPS Publishing.

Brooks, J. G., & Brooks, M. G. (2001). *The case for constructivist classrooms*. Upper Saddle River, NJ: Merrill/Prentice Hall.

Corbett, J. (2001). *Supporting inclusive education: A connective pedagogy*. New York: Routledge/Falmer.

Ormrod, J. E. (2003). *Educational psychology: Developing learners* (4th ed.). Upper Saddle River, NJ: Merrill/Prentice Hall.

Renzulli, J., Gubbins, E. J., McMillen, K. S., Eckert, R. D., & Little, C. A. (Eds.). (2009). *Systems and models for developing programs for the gifted and talented* (2nd ed.). Mansfield Center, CT: Creative Learning Press.

Taylor, R. L., Smiley, L. R., & Richards, S. B. (2009). *Exceptional students: Preparing teachers for the 21st century*. Boston: McGraw-Hill.

Tomlinson, C. A., Kaplan, S. N., Renzulli, J. S., Purcell, J. H., Leppien, J. H., Burns, D. E., et al. (2009). *The parallel curriculum: A design to develop learner potential and challenge advanced learners*. Thousand Oaks, CA: Corwin.

"Discovery Math"

From Professional Development to Classroom Practice

Prereading Focus Points: A veteran math educator has been involved in providing fellow teachers with districtwide professional development opportunities designed to increase awareness of new pedagogies in their content area. However, there are concerns about the degree to which such innovative strategies and materials are actually used in individual classrooms due to a lack of systematic implementation and feedback loop.

Level: School district

Content Area: Mathematics

Setting: Urban, suburban, and rural

Spotlight on . . . Professional development

Key Terms: Discovery learning; project-based learning; action research; balanced curriculum

BACKGROUND INFORMATION ABOUT THE TEACHER

Jane has taught in both areas of her certification—mathematics and vocational business education—for the past 34 years. The district where she teaches was one of the leaders of public education in the nation during the 1950s and 1960s. It comprised students from various economic backgrounds but predominantly middle-class families in which parents were employed by local factories. Each homogeneous neighborhood supported a high school and the feeder elementary and middle schools. There were more than 100,000 students enrolled in this entire public school district. Students were given choices of preparing for a college education and/or vocational training. Over time, because of a poorly administered court order for busing students, enrollment dropped to 70,000 students. Consequently, the school district became predominantly African American. Students were matched according to their economic backgrounds and bused across the city to racially mixed schools.

Vocational programs were moved to magnet schools to better utilize facilities and modern equipment and to encourage a natural mixing of the races by common interests in a vocational program. Many students were highly encouraged to enroll in these programs because they were considered "at risk." This served to "water down" curricula, as well as to discourage able students from enrolling in the programs. The magnet schools were losing enrollment, and graduation rates across the district were plummeting.

After about 16 years, change occurred in the philosophy of the school system. Everyone was expected to receive an education to enable him or her to attend college. Vocational programs dwindled, and Jane was assigned to teach in her other area of certification—mathematics. As a teacher of math, Jane practiced the tried-and-true methods of her teachers—lecturer and memorization of formulas. Jane was passionate about her content area and did always try to connect the math to everyday situations where students would be able to use mathematical skills. She spent a fortune buying supplemental books to provide students with some math investigations into real life.

Then Jane discovered the National Council of Teachers of Mathematics (NCTM) conferences where she learned about the "Discovery Method" of mathematics that ended up changing her whole outlook on the content area. As a visual learner herself, she could actually "see" the mathematics happening. By then she was teaching at the Alternative to Expulsion school and had 7th- to 12th-grade students who had a lot of special needs. The spectrum of mathematical skills was also wide. Jane tried to make math more meaningful for them by using real-life situations and activities from conferences and workshops that she attended. She had very little discipline problems, and students actually worked with her. When the program was disbanded due to lack of funding, Jane was transferred back to a regular high school where she had difficulty teaching for the proficiency test and district math curriculum.

In recent years, Jane became involved in developing some hands-on and discovery materials for teachers to incorporate into their curricula to stimulate students and help them retain mathematical concepts needed for the state graduation test. She also became a regular presenter for NCTM. Additionally, Jane became a supervisor for student interns and practicum students in mathematics. Currently she is a facilitator for Collaborative Excellence workshops organized by a local state university as part of its professional development efforts.

BACKGROUND INFORMATION ABOUT THE CURRICULUM

The curriculum used for the Collaborative Excellence workshops represents a hands-on or discovery learning approach that aligns with state standards and graduation test requirements. Specifically, the curriculum content correlates with the areas of competency designated by the state based on the NCTM model of content areas—data analysis and probability, measurement, geometry, number sense, algebra and functions, and problem solving. Each workshop focuses on a different content area whose competency outcomes are appropriate for grade levels 9 and 10.

> **Discovery learning** is a process in which students acquire knowledge about their physical and/or social environment by engaging in firsthand interactions with its various components.

Teachers from the local county school districts are invited to attend even if they are currently teaching lower grade levels. Special education teachers are also invited. All content areas are covered over the summer during two different weeks. There is an intensive one-week summer session for 4 days, 8 hours per day. Follow-up sessions consisting of one 8-hour day are conducted in the fall and spring. There is also an online WebCT component for teachers to share their experiences using these activities in their classrooms. This is also intended to provide peer support based on which to generate materials and suggestions on usage or adaptations of the materials for different age and/or ability levels.

Each teacher in the workshop completes every activity either with a partner or in a group. Discussions follow the activity, as participants investigate how it could be adapted to various learners. Teachers assume the role of the learner as a way to identify areas of difficulty related to comprehension and/or application.

PROBLEM

Teachers are given materials to use in the classroom, but very few actually do that on a regular basis. They are more likely to use them the day before a holiday or school break to fill in time. It is hard to get teachers to move away from lecturing mode or teacher-directed classroom instruction. Students may work collaboratively in groups, but they appear to be merely sharing answers to problems, not really "discovering" any mathematical information.

Project-based learning involves students in complex and interdisciplinary authentic learning tasks that require higher-level thinking, communication, and collaborative skills, prompted by a range of formative assessment tools.

Additional problems have to do with the following: insufficient/inappropriate use of technology, low expectations on the part of both students and teachers, homework not assigned because "students do not want to do any of that," and no project-based learning opportunities that relate mathematical learning in the classroom to real-life applications.

PROBING QUESTIONS

1. How could the workshop sequence be enhanced to prompt teachers to model some of the strategies and activities to their students?

2. How could these participating teachers be assisted in successfully implementing what they learn during the workshops?

PROPOSED SOLUTION

Since there is a support system in place for teachers who are participating in the Collaborative Excellence workshops, retention of information can be maximized in the following ways:

- Develop a reward system for teachers who try some of the lessons and post their findings on WebCT for their cohorts to see and comment on.
- Tailor follow-up sessions during the next semester to the needs expressed by participants. Any subsequent sessions could vary in number and topics; they could also be used as a venue for dissemination of effective practices based on the initial workshops.
- Increase the involvement of district-level and school-level curriculum coordinators in publicizing the workshops. At the same time, these individuals could determine short-, medium-, and long-term needs of mathematics teachers in their district as a way to design upcoming workshops.

As far as the evidence of successfully implementing strategies and activities learned during the workshops, WebCT provides a foundational platform for exchanges of information. In addition to monitoring the threaded conversations in the online environment, topical or thematic modules could be created to respond to issues raised by participating teachers as a result of their attempts to improve practice in the classroom. Joint projects could lead to collaborative planning for hands-on mathematics lessons and units to be taught at different school sites. Action research ideas could be pursued as a way to disseminate findings related to changes in the pedagogy of mathematics teaching as well as relevant, sustainable student learning.

Action research represents one aspect of recent educational reform efforts aimed at empowering teachers as researchers in their own classroom environment, thus bringing together relevant theory and effective practice.

EXPECTED OUTCOMES

Once teachers have begun to utilize the activities presented during the workshops and share their own successes in implementing them, they should become more confident about creating further learning opportunities for their students. In addition to generating a database of innovative pedagogy supporting an increase in student learning, there will be other related advantages to come out of this: greater student motivation, better student retention of information, more students passing the state graduation test with higher scores, and an increased satisfaction on the part of both teachers and students.

POINTS TO PONDER . . .

Jane has been involved in districtwide efforts to bring mathematics teachers together to investigate appropriate ways to engage students in "discovering" math by means of (inter)active activities. Considering the complex concept of a "balanced curriculum" (Squires, 2009), what kinds of recommendations would you make to support math curriculum effectiveness by planning teaching staff development based on an accurate record of teachers' comments.

A **balanced curriculum** features a strong correlation among standards, subject matter content, and assessment based on a structure that allows for monitoring of student progress, teacher input, and curriculum revisions.

QUESTIONS FOR ADMINISTRATORS

As a school administrator, how would you motivate teachers to become involved in workshops similar to the Collaborative Excellence? What kind of a reward system would you develop and use? How would your plan differ depending on the overall academic standing of your school according to state designation—excellent, effective, continuous improvement, academic watch, or academic emergency?

IN-CLASS ACTIVITY

In self-selected groups assume the role of a school leader. In that capacity, brainstorm ideas related to possible means by which your math teachers would be involved in Collaborative Excellence workshops. Specifically, come up with a plan supporting the implementation, evaluation, and dissemination of findings from individual classrooms to improve student achievement in terms of mathematical knowledge and skills. At the same time, pay attention to how this plan should address some of the secondary issues mentioned by Jane, such as use of instructional technology, student expectations, homework, and opportunities for project-based learning. Prepare a group presentation highlighting your group proposal.

REFERENCE

Squires, D. A. (2009). *Curriculum alignment: Research-based strategies for increasing student achievement*. Thousand Oaks, CA: Corwin.

SUGGESTED READINGS

Kauchak, D. P., & Eggen, P. D. (2007). *Learning and teaching: Research-based methods* (5th ed.). Boston: Allyn & Bacon.

Parkway, F. W., Hass, G., & Anctil, E. J. (2010). *Curriculum leadership: Readings for developing quality educational programs* (9th ed.). Boston: Allyn & Bacon.

Posner, G. J. (2004). *Analyzing the curriculum* (3rd ed.). New York: McGraw-Hill.

Tomlinson, C. A., & McTighe, J. (2006). *Integrating differentiated instruction and understanding by design*. Alexandria, VA: Association for Supervision and Curriculum Development.

Student Understandings as a Basis for Motivation and Participation in a Severe Emotional Disturbance/Severe Behavioral Handicap High School Classroom

Prereading Focus Points: Because of a marked deficiency in the reading ability level of the students in a self-contained high school classroom, there is no formal curriculum being used. Additionally, students' severe emotional and behavioral problems impact the degree to which they perform and achieve in their social studies class. The teacher is faced with a dual dilemma related to decreasing off-task behavior while increasing student motivation and participation in instructional activities.

Level: High school

Content Area: Social studies

Setting: Urban

Spotlight on . . .
  a) Special education;
  b) Off-task behavior; and
  c) Student motivation.

Key Terms: Positive reinforcement systems; essential questions and enduring understandings

BACKGROUND INFORMATION ABOUT THE TEACHER

Alburn School is a high school in an urban school district serving more than 1,200 students mostly coming from the lowest socioeconomic bracket in the country. The school is located in an area featuring housing projects where most of the students reside. There is little diversity at the school, with the student population being almost 100% African American. Gang activity is prevalent both in the community and in the school.

The teaching staff is very diverse, representing Hispanic, Indian, African American, and Caucasian backgrounds. One teacher, Jenny, has been teaching students with severe emotional disturbance/severe behavior handicap (SED/SBH) for 32 years. The students in her classroom are diagnosed SED or SBH and are serviced based on Individualized Education Plans (IEPs). This is a self-contained classroom with students receiving almost 100% of their education in this room. All students are African American; seven of them are male and five female. Most students come from alternative education programs or juvenile detention settings. Additionally, most of them have parole officers (POs).

BACKGROUND INFORMATION ABOUT THE CURRICULUM

The daily routine for Jenny's social studies class features two main components: (a) bellwork, to be completed within the first 10 minutes of class time, and (b) the lesson of the day, to be engaged in following bellwork. Bellwork usually consists of one or two questions related to a real-life issue focusing on basic skills. The rest of class time consists of a reading activity, usually from a printed worksheet based on which students initiate an activity resulting in a wide range of products: posters, mobiles, bulletin boards, or crossword puzzles inclusive of the historical information presented in the assigned readings.

All of these readings align with the state content standards for social studies. However, it should be mentioned that this class does not have a planned/designed curriculum, meaning that students do not use any textbook. The main reason for that has to do with the fact that the textbook offered by the school district is rated at the 9th-/10th-grade reading level, while Jenny's students are between a 2nd-grade and a 6th-grade reading level. Because of the lack of a planned social studies curriculum following a particular sequence, topics are not delineated according to any historical timeline and jump from one time period to another very much at random.

PROBLEM

Students are exhibiting off-task behavior as they talk without permission, which is correlated to their low work productivity. Some of them display off-task behavior by putting their heads on the desk, attempting to take a nap during class. When asked what seems to be the problem preventing them from proceeding with their in-class task, their usual answer has to do with "being bored" and/or not caring about the material being presented to them. They also express a lack of understanding of any prerequisite information pertaining to historical contexts that would help them comprehend any current reading material.

PROBING QUESTIONS

1. How could SED/SBH students be motivated to achieve both academically and socially?

2. How could Jenny reduce the incidence of off-task behavior in her social studies class?

PROPOSED SOLUTION

Jenny should consider the following sequence in planning for a curriculum that would engage students in more meaningful learning that takes into account objectives and outcomes grounded in content area standards:

a) Deliver information in a historical timeline context.

   - Align the information with its respective standards and benchmarks while continuing to present material along the logical timeline of events, which would help students keep their own timeline for the entire semester.
   - Build upon concepts previously discussed by using prior knowledge to help build connections between old and new information.

b) Have students use various strategies to develop an understanding of the information presented.

   - Use a wide range of grouping strategies that allow for both individual work and collaborative efforts.

- Select and utilize online resources, such as www.history.com, to enhance learning.
- Encourage students to create KWL (Know, Want to Know, Learned) charts using a variety of strategies designed to diversify instruction, such as Summarize-Question-Respond (SQR), RAFT (Resource Area for Teaching), Elkonin boxes, Save the Last Word for Me, Before-During-After (BDA), WebQuest, and so forth.
- Involve each student in a microteaching session focused on a single historical concept to be introduced to the rest of the class.
- Use lecturing as a supportive strategy, not the primary means of delivering instruction.

c) Connect the curriculum to student understanding.

- Use real-world examples that students would understand as a way to clarify concepts. For example, when discussing the parts of the Constitution, the articles and amendments, use a neighborhood recreation facility as a parallel. The articles could be like the main parts of the building—the weight room, the gym, activity rooms, and so forth. The amendments are the add-ons or changes to the structure due to the changing needs of the facility. Draw the structure on a transparency, labeling the recreation facility parts, and then follow up by having students come up to label the parts that would be comparable to the Constitution articles and amendments. By taking something concrete that students can see and tying it to abstract ideas, more connections could be created, thus leading to a better understanding of the material.

d) Have students re-create a historical situation in the form of a performance in front of an audience, after which learners could either write about what this all means or critique the performance in a peer review format. This would address requirements related to both English-language arts and social studies. Additionally, visual students would be prompted to see the historical situation, while auditory and tactile learners would have their learning preferences met by the reenactment of the situation.

e) Use appropriate assessment tools to demonstrate student learning. Pre- and postassessment should be used regularly. Scoring rubrics should accompany all assignments so that criteria for assessment are clear to students and teachers alike.

As far as student behavior is concerned, Jenny could consider the following:

f) Have students complete an interest inventory to determine important intrinsic rewards to each student in class. This kind of information could be used to create a token economy system that combines primary and secondary reinforcers with activity reinforcers.

g) Determine target behaviors for rewards; consistently follow the reward program in a way that highlights both logical consequences to inappropriate behavior and a wide range of rewards for desired behaviors.

EXPECTED OUTCOMES

- By aligning the curriculum with a timeline, students should be able to demonstrate a better understanding of the historical sequence of events they study. Moreover, the use of their own timeline will help them see what they have learned and where the new information fits into the developing topic- or theme-related schema.

- The lack of intrinsic interest in learning should decrease because of the diversification of the learning styles and variation in delivery of material making the class more interesting.

- Learning should also increase because of the fact that the various learning styles are being fostered. At the same time, learning can be accurately measured through the use of pre- and postassessment tools that clarify expectations of both the learning and the assessment cycles.

> **Positive reinforcement systems** represent programs designed to reward desired or acceptable student behavior by means of positive consequences to the behavior in question.

- Off-task behavior should decrease due to more interest in curriculum as well as the positive reinforcement system based upon students' interests in the content areas.

POINTS TO PONDER . . .

Given the fact that Jenny's students do not use a formal curriculum, consider how you would recommend that she use "essential questions" and "enduring understandings" (Wiggins & McTighe, 2005) designed to lead to sustainable acquisition of knowledge and development of skills. Moreover, factor in the ability levels of her students and how they impact the sequencing of her social studies class content.

> **Essential questions** lead to the uncovering of the complexity of an academic discipline by means of inquiry on the part of students. **Enduring understandings** transfer knowledge ("big ideas") beyond the realm of the classroom.

The next step would be to think of the developmentally appropriate instructional resources Jenny could use to motivate her students and ensure meaningful learning. How would she be able to provide students with stimuli that lead to achievement both academically and in terms of positive social skills?

QUESTIONS FOR ADMINISTRATORS

How would you involve Jenny, as well as other special and general education teachers, in conversations about appropriate ways to provide students with developmentally appropriate access to curriculum? What do you think could be done to narrow the gap between the actual reading ability level and the expected performance level mentioned by Jenny? How would you monitor the development, implementation, and evaluation of individualized curriculum goals for such students?

IN-CLASS ACTIVITY

In self-selected groups, determine an assessment plan that Jenny could use in her social studies class. Identify the "right" balance between formative and summative assessment tools. Which of them would be more conducive to increased student motivation and participation in classroom activities? Who else should be involved in the design phase? What suggestions would you have for the evaluation of the assessment plan's effectiveness? Prepare a brief group presentation highlighting several "tips from the experts" that Jenny could use right away.

REFERENCE

Wiggins, G., & McTighe, J. (2005). *Understanding by design* (2nd ed.). Upper Saddle River, NJ: Pearson.

SUGGESTED READINGS

Armstrong, T. (2006). *The best schools: How human development research should inform educational practice.* Alexandria, VA: Association for Supervision and Curriculum Development.

Hardin, C. J. (2008). *Effective classroom management: Models and strategies for today's classrooms* (2nd ed.). Upper Saddle River, NJ: Merrill/Prentice Hall.

Nolet, V., & McLaughlin, M. J. (2005). *Accessing the general curriculum: Including students with disabilities in standards-based reform* (2nd ed.). Thousand Oaks, CA: Sage.

Passe, J. (1996). *When students choose content: A guide to increasing motivation, autonomy, and achievement.* Thousand Oaks, CA: Corwin.

Popham, W. J. (2008). *Transformative assessment.* Alexandria, VA: Association for Supervision and Curriculum Development.

Price, H. B. (2008). *Mobilizing the community to help students succeed.* Alexandria, VA: Association for Supervision and Curriculum Development.

Scheuermann, B. K., & Hall, J. A. (2008). *Positive behavioral supports for the classroom.* Upper Saddle River, NJ: Merrill/Prentice Hall.

Meeting Student Learning Requirements by Means of an Improved Writing-Across-Curriculum Program

Prereading Focus Points: Collaboration among teachers may not always lead to the effective implementation of an interdisciplinary program focusing on a particular set of skills (such as writing). School administrators are charged with leading teachers to find appropriate ways in which to motivate students, relate to their interests, and evidence learning on a continuous basis.

Level: Middle school

Content Area: English-language arts

Setting: Urban

Spotlight on . . .

   a) Authentic assessment;
   b) Writing across curriculum; and
   c) Differentiation.

Key Terms: Assessment mapping; authentic assessment

BACKGROUND INFORMATION ABOUT THE TEACHER

Kim has been an assistant principal at Triskett Middle School for the past 5 years. Her school is a seventh- and eighth-grade building consisting of approximately 650 students and 80 teachers/staff. The school, located in the Rockford City School District, is an outer-ring school of a large metropolitan area. The school is considered urban with about 80% of the population being African American, 17% White, and 3% other. The majority of the staff is Caucasian. Approximately 65% of Triskett students receive free or reduced lunch and breakfast. The classes consist of a mix of inclusion students, regular education students, and a multiple-disability population. The school suffers from a lack of parental involvement when it comes to curricular events organized by the school. Approximately 25% of the parents attend conferences and open-house events. Kim has been attempting to blend her background knowledge in English-language arts with recent research findings on school leadership that she learned about in her own graduate-level courses. Her efforts are intended to engage her colleagues in making curricular decisions based on assessment data analysis in a way that would enhance the existing writing curriculum.

BACKGROUND INFORMATION ABOUT THE CURRICULUM

It seems that, regardless of the various initiatives and professional development opportunities, teachers use lectures as a favorite presentation mode, while information processing, on the part of students, relies solely on traditional paper-and-pencil assessment tools. With this in mind, norm-reference tests are given to students to determine the degree to which learning has occurred based on a Holt McDougal textbook.

Assessment mapping is the procedure that outlines the connections among assessment tools, student performance, and the instructional activities designed to help students meet set objectives.

Assessment mapping has been initiated as a way to address the fact that there is very little room for authentic assessment in the current planned curriculum. Kim fears that traditional assessment will continue to be used almost exclusively, thus limiting the opportunities for writing across disciplines.

The assessment mapping collaborative effort is also intended to investigate the actual ways in which multicultural learning actually takes place at Triskett Middle School. Building teachers seem to believe that a few multicultural experiences are enough to create a feeling of unity. Consequently, outside resources are rarely tapped into as a way to meet the needs of the diverse student population. Along the same lines, although the language arts curriculum calls for advanced classes as well as inclusion classes, very little is accomplished to differentiate the instruction of these students. Each inclusion class has a special education teacher, but the curriculum and the assessment materials are typically the same for all students, regardless of which class they attend. By law, students are required to receive differentiated instruction molded to their various needs, and the "teacher's job is to teach to that variety, that diversity" (Ayers, 2001 p. 16).

> **Authentic assessment** provides evidence of relevant correlations between classroom-based learning and opportunities for application of knowledge to real-life situations.

For the second year of school improvement, state coaches have been assigned in Academic Yearly Progress (AYP) areas, such as math and reading, to help facilitate the proper use of the 84-minute time blocks and to focus on effective teaching and learning.

PROBLEM

Triskett Middle School posts annual scores below expectations on the state achievement tests in math and reading. Upon evaluation of the assessment data by school principals and teachers, students appear to do poorly on short-answer items as well as on extended-response essay prompts on both exams. A high percentage of students either do not answer the questions or receive a score of zero. The analysis of this trend led school personnel to believe that students were uncomfortable answering these types of test items and would not even attempt them.

The whole school has gone to an 84-minute block of time to put a greater emphasis on reading across curriculum, especially math and English. Because Triskett is in its second year of school improvement, interventions have been put into place to accommodate some of the troubled areas for these two curricula.

As Triskett stands today, students are taught what they don't know. "The curriculum is built on a deficit model; it is built on repairing weakness. And it simply doesn't work" (Ayers, 2001, p. 31). The problem stems from a need to shift the focus of instruction to *how* students learn. There is no question that the data clearly show writing to be an area in which students are struggling. In her capacity as a school administrator, Kim believes that the solution to the problem lies in changing how writing is taught. At the same time, the planned/designed curriculum proven not to be working for all individuals to be successful needs to be revised.

PROBING QUESTIONS

1. How could the curriculum mapping exercise be used to strengthen the existing writing curriculum?

2. How could the inclusion of culturally relevant activities in the curriculum be increased in ways that support differentiated instruction?

ACTUAL SOLUTION

The lack of teaching strategies emphasizing writing and differentiation has produced the same poor results year after year. In an attempt to eradicate the problem and get all teachers on board with the same writing techniques, the Formula Writing model was recommended. Formula Writing is a structured approach to sentence and paragraph building that reveals the underlying architecture inherent in good writing. The model was expected to provide a framework for all teachers to use writing in each class.

First, several teachers were selected to see a colleague of theirs model the appropriate use of Formula Writing. Her ideas and procedures were then disseminated to the other teaching staff members. Additionally, a professional development in-service on the model was given to all teachers during a workday. Each teacher was given resources based on the principles of the Formula Writing model and given guidance on implementation.

The charge was given that writing was to be done daily by students in each subject area. Every area was designated a specific day so that students would be writing at least once daily. Teachers were encouraged to use several resources to incorporate writing into their curriculum. The districtwide writing initiative was designed to ensure that all students were getting familiar and comfortable with the style of writing. At the same time, the expectations from grade to grade would be consistent across the district as far as writing proficiency was concerned.

Ellen came to Triskett Middle School to work directly with teachers and 630 students in an assembly-like format. She took them by grade levels, 315 students at a time, and gave several examples of Formula Writing, after which teachers and students were prompted to ask questions.

According to the Formula Writing model, the procedural steps to be used are as follows:

1. Students are presented with either a question or a situation, based on which they have to decide what is being asked of them (what the task is).

2. Students draw a wheel in the middle of which they place the topic under discussion or the answer needed to the question asked by the teacher.

3. In a logical sequence, students are to draw a number of spokes connected to the middle of the wheel (represented by the topic being discussed or the answer needed) where they would place examples, facts, or reasons to support the answer being sought.

4. Students are then asked to draw another set of spokes representing "snap words," such as *and* and/or *because*, which require details and elaboration. For instance, by answering the question "What happened?" and adding *and* in the snap spoke, students have to continue the description of the event. By answering the question "What do you know about _____?" and adding *because* in the snap spoke, students have to provide evidence of their knowledge of the given topic.

5. Now students begin writing by generating a topic sentence starting with the word(s) in the middle of the wheel, after which they proceed by defining or explaining the topic/answer.

6. Progressively, students turn each spoke into a complete sentence by means of the "snap words" that function as logical connectors.

This model of writing engages students in the writing process across the whole curriculum by providing them with relevant topics/questions and prompts such as "snap it!" or "punch it with punctuation!" Consequently, Triskett Middle School students became interested in the process of writing as it was generating fun activities designed to build skills. At the same time, teachers were able to incorporate a variety of resources and purposes for writing, as opposed to simply following a linear approach to a writing curriculum as a separate entity. These resources would necessarily integrate writing prompts meant to encourage students to investigate their cultural and ethnic identities (Noel, 2000) as well as those of others. In this case, the interdisciplinary approach to writing across curriculum would become transformative by enabling "students to view concepts, issues, events, and themes from the perspectives of diverse ethnic and cultural groups" (Banks & Banks, 2004, p. 246).

Equally important, all teachers were on the same page in terms of evaluation of student work collected by means of authentic assessment tools. Rubrics were used to formally/objectively interpret writing skills. Concurrently, the flexibility in the districtwide implementation of this model made it possible for differentiation to be used so that students could develop an appreciation for writing while being held accountable for the same levels of performance.

OBSERVED OUTCOMES

The most important expectation had to do with the increase in the percentage of students successfully attempting to answer writing prompts on the state achievement test. Teachers were also able to identify additional resources to support the whole process of writing across curriculum. For all this to happen, professional development opportunities had to be offered on a continuous basis so that there was sufficient "buy-in" and momentum to maintain the gains in student writing skills.

Since this was a districtwide initiative, there had to be appropriate administrative support and evaluation of the ways in which the writing-across-curriculum model was being implemented at different school sites. Regular team meetings were coupled with opportunities for teachers and students to showcase their progress in using the model. At the same time, all teachers involved in the districtwide project continued their collaborative work in terms of the appropriate ways in which the students' writing skills could be improved once the model would no longer be needed.

Another very important outcome emphasized the opportunity students had to integrate multiculturalism in their learning process by being able to write about topics that interested them. In this light, samples of student work were disseminated throughout the district as a way to demonstrate best skill-building practices integrating writing skills in various content areas.

POINTS TO PONDER . . .

In her capacity as a school administrator, Kim is faced with the dilemma of engaging her teaching staff in productive conversations about strengthening the process of writing across curriculum. Which approach should Kim use to encourage curriculum change in her school—"directive-control" (school leader assigns plan of action, minimal teacher autonomy), "directive-informational" (school leader offers range of choices from which teachers choose a particular one), "collaborative" (plans of action are determined and selected collaboratively), or "nondirective" (teachers are in control of the planning process, maximum teacher autonomy) (Glickman, 2002, pp. 42–43.)? How should the school assessment plan be designed so that it aligns data from authentic assessment tools with specific student and teacher accountability requirements? What dissemination and professional development plan should be used to maximize teacher "buy-in"? Furthermore, how could teachers and students develop a sense of ownership of the experienced curriculum focused on writing across the various content areas?

QUESTIONS FOR SCHOOL ADMINISTRATORS

How would you involve faculty and staff in a curriculum mapping exercise aimed to identify interdisciplinary units, themes, or modules at a grade level of your choice? Also, how would you use assessment data to inform faculty about the need to refocus instruction onto "how students learn," thus emphasizing student learning as a process rather than a collection of end products?

IN-CLASS EXERCISE

In content-area or grade-level groups, based on a scenario provided by your course instructor, discuss how you would "map out" the connections between the leadership styles mentioned earlier and various teaching strategies as they tie to specific student learning assessment data (as demonstrated by state report cards or any other set of information from the public domain). How strong should these connections be for a school to demonstrate continuous improvement as well as a leadership style supportive of it? Prepare an interactive group presentation that would be the source of a whole-class list of leadership and teaching strategies identified to promote increased learning.

REFERENCES

Ayers, W. (2001). *To teach: The journey of a teacher*. New York: Teachers College Press.

Banks, J. A., & Banks, C. A. M. (Eds.). (2004). *Multicultural education: Issues and perspectives* (5th ed.). Hoboken, NJ: Wiley.

Glickman, C. D. (2002). *Leadership for learning: How to help teachers succeed*. Alexandria, VA: Association for Supervision and Curriculum Development.

Noel, J. (2000). *Developing multicultural educators*. Long Grove, IL: Waveland Press, Inc.

SUGGESTED READINGS

Chiarelott, L. (2006). *Curriculum in context: Designing curriculum for teaching and learning in context*. Belmont, CA: Thomson Wadsworth.

Jacobs, H. H. (Ed.). (2004). *Getting results with curriculum mapping*. Alexandria, VA: Association for Supervision and Curriculum Development.

Reeves, D. B. (2006). *The learning leader: How to focus school improvement for better results*. Alexandria, VA: Association for Supervision and Curriculum Development.

CASE 10

Student Portfolios and Authentic Assessment in a Diverse Multiage Preschool Classroom

Prereading Focus Points: Implementing a planned curriculum requires teachers to make accommodations to meet the specific needs of their students. Teaching literacy to a diverse multiage classroom relies on complex measures designed to determine student progress. Concomitantly, providing students with opportunities for hands-on learning relates to individual differences.

Level: Preschool

Content area: English-language arts

Setting: Urban

Spotlight on . . .

a) Developmentally appropriate instruction;
b) Authentic assessment; and
c) Cooperative learning.

Key Terms: Oliva model; Even Start Family Literacy programs

BACKGROUND INFORMATION ABOUT THE TEACHER

Elaine is a teacher at Heights Even Start in Moreland Heights. Even Start is a family literacy program with four components—adult education (General Educational Development [GED] and English for Speakers of Other Languages [ESOL]), parenting classes, parent and child together, and early childhood. To be eligible for the program, the parent needs to be enrolled in either GED classes or English classes and have a child up to age 8. Elaine is a teacher in a diverse multiage preschool class. Her students range in age from 3 to 5, and almost half of the students have very limited English proficiency. Heights Even Start is a partnership of the Moreland Heights School District and is funded through a grant by the state department of education.

BACKGROUND INFORMATION ABOUT THE CURRICULUM

Elaine uses the Let's Begin With the Letter People curriculum. Let's Begin is a comprehensive curriculum organized around themes that integrate knowledge across subject areas. The curriculum focuses on oral language, print awareness, phonological and phonemic awareness, alphabetic knowledge, writing, and vocabulary development. Let's Begin demonstrates a clear distinction among aims, goals, and objectives. It also incorporates daily content learning activities and provides its own assessment tools. The curriculum also has a statement of philosophy like in the Oliva models (1976, 1992) based on strongly held beliefs of early childhood educators, which are stated in the "Blueprint for Learning" that comes with the curriculum. Elaine also follows the state Early Learning Content Standards, which describe essential concepts and skills for young children to learn and do in the areas of English-language arts, mathematics, social studies, and science.

> **Oliva** proposes a model for curriculum development featuring a sequence of steps ranging from curriculum goals developed based on various sources of information to a final curriculum evaluation through several planning and operational phases.

> **Even Start Family Literacy programs** partner schools and their communities in an attempt to address issues such as poverty and illiteracy by means of aligning early childhood education, adult literacy, and parenting education.

Most of her instruction and activities are literacy based due to the fact that Even Start is a literacy program; however, she does use the Letter People to integrate lessons across all the content areas. The program is evaluated by the state only in the area of English-language arts. Early Childhood Education Performance Indicator 1 states that "100% of children, ages 3–5 (and not in kindergarten), whose families have participated in Even Start for at least four months will demonstrate progress in reading and reading strategies as measured by the assessment called Individual Growth and Development Indicators (IGDI)."

The IGDI assessment administered to Elaine's preschool students is called Get it, Got it, Go! The three early literacy assessments are picture naming, rhyming, and alliteration. IGDIs identify children at risk, evaluate the effectiveness of instruction, and can be used repeatedly. These indicators allow Elaine to measure a child's growth over time toward long-term developmentally appropriate goals, instead of just measuring his or her skill level at one point in time. She can also use a student's data to plot his or her "trend line" to compare how well he or she is progressing compared to children who are typically developing.

PROBLEM

This has been a very challenging year for Elaine. Teaching in any multiage class presents obvious developmental differences between the students, and this creates a very wide range of abilities in the classroom. Many of her students come from disadvantaged families and are considered at risk. Elaine's students are African American, Hispanic, and Asian, with the latter two groups of children being non-English speakers. At the same time, she has no "typical" or "model" students. For various environmental and other factors, many of the students need to be referred to the school psychologist for testing. Two of Elaine's students were already on Individualized Education Plans for behavioral and emotional conditions prior to coming to her classroom, while three more of her students are in the process of being assessed. When observing one of the students in her class, the school psychologist told Elaine that she had a special education class. However, Elaine is not certified in special education.

Elaine's hardest challenge has been attempting to make accommodations in her lesson plans and curriculum to meet the needs of all students. It is difficult and time consuming to do that, so she worries that she is not always able to reach all of them. She tries to do some individualized instruction during center time, but she wishes she could devote more time. It is very hard to take the planned Letter People curriculum and make the modifications to meet the needs of her students. For example, Elaine has a student who can rhyme, identify all the letters of the alphabet, write her name, and read environmental print and who demonstrates an understanding of concepts about print. Sitting right next to her is another child who can't even recognize her name written on a piece of paper.

Often the taught (enacted) curriculum is very different from the planned curriculum. An illustration of this problem in Elaine's classroom occurred at the end of a weeklong theme. Elaine and her students spent the whole week on Ms. W, and the culminating activity was to identify which word did not belong (to pick which word did not have the same initial consonant sound as the rest of the "W" words). She spent the whole week implementing hands-on concrete examples of "W" words such as eating watermelon, reading *Wemberly Worried* and *Mrs. Wishy Washy,* singing "Willaby Wallaby Woo," and going on a word hunt. When it came time to do the culminating activity, two students gave her the answer she was looking for before they had even named the pictures. Her other students were not ready to determine initial consonant or alliteration; this activity was at their frustration level even with teacher assistance. This shows that what is developmentally appropriate for one student in the classroom may not be developmentally appropriate for another student. Sometimes Elaine feels that when teaching a lesson, she is either losing or boring some of the students. Consequently, she ends up supplementing the curriculum with her own enrichment activities, but this is also very time consuming, while it feels a little random, with no structure in place for such accommodations.

PROBING QUESTIONS

1. How could the developmental needs of these students be met by means of differentiated instruction?

2. How could the cultural diversity of students be integrated into teaching in ways that motivate learning?

PROPOSED SOLUTION

While pondering possible solutions, Elaine focused on John Dewey's philosophy of education. Two of his concepts resonating the most with her are the facts that the child should be at the center of his or her education and that students should be active and alert instead of passive and receptive. Dewey (1900/1990) believed that real progress can be measured in the development of new attitudes and that interest in experience and education relies on continually reshaping experience. Elaine's proposed solution to better meet the diverse needs of her students through differentiated instruction is threefold: (1) more opportunities for cooperative learning and individualized instruction, (2) more authentic assessments, and (3) greater attention to cultural awareness and sensitivity.

To be able to provide developmentally appropriate instruction and activities, Elaine needs to determine where each student is on a continuum of knowledge and skills. She decides to make more in-depth use of the Get it, Got it, Go! assessment tools, coupled with the formal assessment from the Letter People curriculum. Together, these assessments will help her pinpoint specific goals according to the individual needs of each child. Elaine also feels that it will be very advantageous to create a goal sheet for each child so that she can become more aware of how well each child is progressing toward important developmental outcomes. Elaine already keeps a portfolio for each child, mostly for parent–teacher conference purposes. Examples of more authentic assessment in the classroom include anecdotal records, observations, checklists, and portfolios. These will allow Elaine to supplement formal assessment scores with occurrences from the everyday classroom, where the child is in a more comfortable, natural setting.

Elaine's teaching experience and graduate-level coursework confirmed that optimal learning takes place when children are involved in a lesson through a variety of hands-on activities. Therefore, she will use the data collected from both formal and informal assessments to create appropriate cooperative learning activities as well as individual instruction. She can introduce concepts by teaching "mini lessons" to the whole class during circle time and then allow for more focused instruction and guided discovery and for learning individually or in groups.

This would aid Elaine in the example of the initial consonant sound activity described before. Due to their wide range of abilities, students would benefit from flexible grouping. She could group students based on their need for additional practice with initial sounds and use the time to provide extra instruction to these students. Another option is to use peer tutoring to group students together so that some students will act as scaffolds to the other students who have not yet mastered the skill (e.g., grouping a student who has not mastered initial sound or repetition with a student who already has). Elaine will also make every effort to schedule more one-on-one instruction during center time. Even if she is only able to work with one or two students a day in the course of 2 weeks, she will likely be able to work individually with each student. Preschool students welcome engaging in an activity with the teacher; it is a wonderful way to build rapport with them all while extending learning opportunities.

Elaine's class is also culturally diverse. She has only nine students, yet four different languages are spoken in the classroom: English, Spanish, Korean, and Japanese. Therefore, she has the task of teaching small children a new language. One of the students is from El Salvador, and Spanish is the language spoken at home. The student's mother approached Elaine one day and told her that her son had mentioned that Elaine only spoke in English to him. She was shocked and somehow felt responsible—the only place he was exposed to English was in Elaine's classroom. Had she somehow felt that Spanish was inferior or unnecessary? Other parents have expressed concerns that learning English and their native tongue at the same time might be confusing to their child. With this in mind, Elaine wonders now if they perceive learning English as cultural change or loss. Often the children learn English at a much more accelerated speed than their parents who are enrolled in ESOL classes, which may explain why the parents may not be comfortable with the fact that their children are learning English and becoming "Americanized." One student is from Japan. Her mother says that since coming to the United States the student doesn't want to eat Japanese food; now her food of choice is hot dogs. Elaine needs to make certain that she and all her students are aware of and sensitive to other cultures, while celebrating their differences. The key for optimal learning is for the children to be in a nurturing, risk-free environment first. This starts by acknowledging the different cultures, through posters, books, music, dolls, and food in the dramatic play area. Children should see different cultures being equally represented. Elaine has already gone to the library and taken out CDs that have counting in Spanish and Japanese. At circle time, students count in everyone's language and are learning together how to say words like *sunny* or *rainy* in different languages. Elaine ordered more bilingual books and did a whole unit on folk tales from around the world.

Banks and Banks (2004) describe how to successfully establish relationships of trust and respect between teachers and students in the classroom. According to these authors, sensitive multicultural pedagogy is one foundation for such trust. If students and teachers alike can realize that everyone is multicultural, then safe "third spaces" can be established to explore the relationship with both new and old cultures together.

EXPECTED OUTCOMES

By following the proposed solution, Elaine can expect to better meet the needs of all her students. By using more assessment strategies, she will be able to tailor her instruction to meet the developmental goals set for each student. Creating an environment that allows for various daily meaningful and purposeful literacy experiences will also actively engage the learners.

Providing individual instruction and cooperative learning activities will enable students to construct and reconstruct their learning experiences. By acknowledging the importance of culture in education, Elaine can create a community of learners, whereby everyone works together to achieve common goals. In *The Passionate Teacher*, Fried (2001, p. 124) states, "The Game of School begins to change when we acknowledge one another's uniqueness."

POINTS TO PONDER . . .

Elaine deals with a set of curricular problems related to using relevant assessment data to differentiate her instruction in ways that engage students in cooperative learning opportunities in an interdisciplinary literacy program connecting schools and family/community environments. How would you manage the process of forming, maintaining, and evaluating group work in a classroom setting as diverse as Elaine's? How would you ensure the transfer of knowledge and skills from the classroom to the "real-life" setting of the students' family/community environment? How would you increase parental involvement in a school-family literacy partnership program while keeping "the focus on children" (Price, 2008, p. 102) in a way that leads to "de-tracking" (Oakes & Lipton, 2007, p. 319)?

QUESTIONS FOR ADMINISTRATORS

Keeping in mind the diverse and multiage structure of Elaine's classroom, how would you correlate your teachers' efforts to differentiate their curricula with the parents' participation in a school-family-based partnership program? How would you support the creation and maintenance of "communities of practice" (Kroll et al., 2005, p. 107)?

IN-CLASS ACTIVITY

As a whole class, brainstorm for ideas related to how you would use student portfolios to document both student learning and awareness of multiculturalism. How would you evaluate such portfolio artifacts? What role would family/community play in the evaluation process? As a follow-up to this preparatory activity, form groups within which to prepare a sample outline of the structure of such a student portfolio along with a brief description of its implementation in a classroom as diverse as Elaine's.

REFERENCES

Banks, J. A., & Banks, C. A. M. (Eds.). (2004). *Multicultural education: Issues and perspectives* (5th ed.). Hoboken, NJ: Wiley.

Dewey, J. (1990). *The school and society. The child and the curriculum.* Chicago: University of Chicago Press. (Original works published 1900, 1902)

Fried, R. L. (2001). *The passionate teacher: A practical guide* (2nd ed.). Boston: Beacon Press.

Kroll, L. R., Cossey, R., Donahue, D. M., Galguera, T., LaBoskey, V. K., Richert, A. E., et al. (2005). *Teaching as principled practice: Managing complexity for social justice.* Thousand Oaks, CA: Sage.

Oakes, J., & Lipton, M. (2007). *Teaching to change the world* (3rd ed.). New York: McGraw-Hill.

Oliva, P. F. (2009). *Developing the curriculum* (7th ed.). Boston: Allyn & Bacon.

Price, H. B. (2008). *Mobilizing the community to help students succeed*. Alexandria, VA: Association for Supervision and Curriculum Development.

SUGGESTED READINGS

Brooks, J. G., & Brooks, M. G. (1999). *In search of understanding: The case for constructivist classrooms*. Upper Saddle River, NJ: Merrill/Prentice Hall.

Corbett, J. (2001). *Supporting inclusive education: A connective pedagogy*. New York: Routledge/Falmer.

Hill, J. D., & Flynn, K. M. (2006). *Classroom instruction that works with English language learners*. Alexandria, VA: Association for Supervision and Curriculum Development.

Littky, D., & Grabelle, S. (2004). *The big picture: Education is everyone's picture*. Alexandria, VA: Association for Supervision and Curriculum Development.

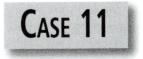

Skill Building in Elementary Math

Between Remediation and Academic Promotion

Prereading Focus Points: Quite often teachers face the challenge of having to remedy the lack of prior knowledge and skills from which to engage their students in the grade level–appropriate curriculum sequence. In addition to having to deal with time constraints derived from standards-based curriculum requirements, teachers also have to identify relevant ways in which to identify early on what students already know and are able to do as a result of having moved up from one grade level to the next.

Level: Elementary

Content Area: Mathematics

Setting: Rural

Spotlight on . . .

a) Standards-based education;
b) Curriculum adaptations (in terms of time and resources); and
c) Skill-building remedial work.

Key Terms: Title I programs; Walker's deliberative approach

BACKGROUND INFORMATION ABOUT THE TEACHER

It is a Tuesday morning in early September: the first day of classes for Lida, who teaches third- and fourth-grade Title I math in a rural middle-class school district. She has been working out her schedule for the first 2 weeks of

Title I programs aim to support schools serving a high number or percentage of students coming from impoverished backgrounds by providing them with opportunities to meet the challenges of academic standards.

school, and today is the day she will start pulling her students out of their classes to work with them in small groups.

Lida has been a teacher for 13 years, working from kindergarten to eighth grade in many districts, in both public and private settings. She feels that she is creative and experienced in the classroom. The district contains three grade-level elementary schools. One of the schools houses kindergarten through second grade, another one third and fourth grades, and the last one fifth and sixth grades. There are approximately 2,000 children in grades K–6 in this particular rural middle-class district in the northeastern corner of the state. There are about 70 teachers and staff employed at the elementary level. Lida is excited about the opportunity to help her 26 new students feel confident and excel in math at the current grade level. She will be meeting with these students for approximately 90 minutes a week broken into two to three segments of 30 to 45 minutes each. This class is meant for students struggling with mathematical concepts recently taught. There are no more than 6 students in a group—usually, these groups accommodate about 4 students.

BACKGROUND INFORMATION ABOUT THE CURRICULUM

Lida bases her lessons on the state content standards for grades 3 and 4. The textbook used in the classroom is published by Scott Foresman, and it is set up in chapters and broken into several lessons within each chapter. Each lesson introduces a mathematical concept, demonstrates how to practice it, and then provides guided practice for students. The traditional, linear sequencing of the third-grade content is demonstrated by the range of chapter topics, as follows:

- Data, graphs, and facts review
- Place, value, and time
- Adding whole numbers and money
- Subtracting whole numbers and money
- Multiplication: concepts and facts
- Division: concepts and facts
- Using geometry to multiply and divide
- Fractions and customary linear measurement
- Decimals and the metric linear measurement
- Measurement and probability

Each of the lessons features three parts: Explore, Connect, and Practice. An example lesson from the third-grade text is Adding with Regrouping. The book shows pictures of how to add two-digit numbers in the Explore part and then uses the pictures and numbers to show how they relate in the Connect part, after which there are approximately 10 to 15 problems in the Practice part, which focuses on adding with regrouping. If more practice is needed, there are an additional 6 problems in the back of the text. The chapters conclude with a review page with 2 to 3 problems from each lesson and then a test as the culminating assessment tool. Lida adapts the curriculum to fit her needs in a particular classroom. She gives more practice on any given skill, if needed. She also uses other resources to provide further practice in areas where her students seem to be struggling.

PROBLEM

Lida gathers the first group of students from two different third-grade classes and takes them to her small yet cozy classroom. For the first part of her lesson she has decided to conduct a review session by using flashcards. She knows that the third graders have not yet learned multiplication facts, so she has combined just the subtraction and addition for them to do. She knows that the children like competition but don't really like the fast pace at which flashcards are traditionally used in the game "Around the World." Lida has decided that she will play the game slightly differently. She will choose a random amount of cards from which one will be shown to each student expected to tell the answer. If the correct answer is given, the student will get to hold the card. When all the cards are gone, the winner will be the one who has the most cards. Lida has planned for the flashcards activity to take about 5 minutes. However, what happens over the next 30 minutes is not what Lida planned. It takes the group of five students about 25 minutes to answer the approximately 35 cards. She doesn't want to pressure them by setting a time limit. She wants them to feel comfortable about using as much time as they need. While waiting for the students to answer, she thinks that they need to brush up on these facts after a long summer break. She watches as many of the students use their fingers or just stare blankly at the card before making an incorrect guess. This discourages her, but she knows it is just because of the lack of practice during the long summer break. She escorts the students back to their classrooms and gathers her next group, also third graders. She starts the same flashcards activity. She finds this group is about the same. As her day continues, with both third and fourth graders she finds that the prior knowledge of math facts is lacking. The students have apparently been passed on to the next grade level without knowing the basics of the grade level they have just passed from. How could that happen? In order to be considered for the Title I program, a student must have two forms of recommendation. One such source of information is the state standardized test's overall math score from the previous year. This score does not show a specific deficit of knowledge of math facts, just an overall deficiency in math. The second source of information is a teacher recommendation. If a student scores 50% or lower on the standardized test, then the homeroom teacher is asked to recommend which children could use the service the most.

After working for a few weeks with all her groups and seeing little progress in the facts area, Lida begins using a new assessment strategy that she designed. In addition to the drilling exercise using flashcards, she starts a combination of oral/written work she calls "math drill." This uses a chart that has 11 boxes. Above the column of 11 boxes the child writes down the number that he or she is on (each child starts at 0 and moves up from there as much as he or she can). Lida calls out the numbers between 0 and 10 in no particular order, and the students have to add or multiply the number at the top of their column by the number the teacher says. When the children complete a column correctly twice, then they move on to the next number. This helps her realize where the problem is with each child. Some of her fourth graders are unable to get past multiplying by 3s.

The problem that Lida faces will most likely continue to be a problem and probably will get worse as the year continues. More advanced mathematical concepts will be difficult to master, as the basic facts are not learned. It seems that students are not being held accountable for their own learning and therefore are going to get farther behind each year they are allowed to do that. Therefore, teachers must consistently review prior knowledge and skills with these students, while both impacting the overall progress made and trying to stick to the mandated curriculum time frame.

PROBING QUESTIONS

1. How would you address the issue of prior knowledge and skills that do not support academic promotion to the next grade level?

2. How could you identify problem areas as well as students with content area deficiencies ahead of time so that remediation can be effective and timely?

PROPOSED SOLUTION

The solution would involve forming a content-area committee to review the current curriculum and how the current text supports it. It may involve tweaking the current curriculum to place a heavier emphasis on skill-building opportunities for students. This focus on common mathematical skills would ensure an increased degree of consistency from grade level to grade level as well as from classroom to classroom within the same grade level. Also, the quality of instruction could be judged against a common core of expectations related to student learning in the Title I program.

The curriculum implementation is similar to Taba's (1962) inverted model, where there are eight steps that move from needs assessment to the overall balance of the different curricular components. Following the identification of needs, specific objectives are developed, based on which content is selected and organized. Learning opportunities (the actual lesson and the use of relevant examples), materials (manipulatives), teacher activities (teachers show examples to class), student activities (students practice the skill assisted by the teacher), and test activities (students prove they have learned the particular skill) represent the next logical steps in the process. The final step is a summative analysis of how such a sequence led to well-balanced connections between all the curricular components mentioned earlier.

Under these circumstances, the new system would also need to include more creative objectives and multiple outcomes. Just as Eisner (1979) wanted educators to start with the end in mind and work from there, Lida would have to be creative in the ways she connects prior knowledge to new content. This implies the inclusion of objectives that take into account the specific pace at which students learn, as opposed to using exclusively preset objectives. Equally important, the range of instructional strategies should include the proper means of differentiation, particularly useful in Lida's teaching environment. At the same time, the means students use to demonstrate learning should also be flexible and accommodating of the particulars of their learning processes. Some ideas may be to have small-group lessons for the children who need it, make picture clues to go along with each fact, and post a bulletin board with some more difficult facts on it so the students can study them at any free moment. Lida could encourage and even offer prizes for learned facts. She could print flashcards for each of the students who don't know the facts to use both at school in free time and at home.

In this light, the team of content-area teachers should analyze the correlation between the standards in their area of expertise and the content supporting the teaching and learning process in the classroom. In other words, the use of formal, standardized assessment tools (derived from the content standards) should be coupled with a frequent implementation of formative and diagnostic assessment designed to provide teachers with accurate information about the progress of all students at any point in time. This type of "assessment for learning" (Stiggins, Arter, Chappuis, & Chappuis, 2006, p. 31) does more than just produce evidence of learning—it enhances it.

EXPECTED OUTCOMES

Students would have a better understanding of the mathematical knowledge and skills that are expected to be mastered at each of the grade levels, according to state standards. Equally important, students need to be held accountable for their learning in each grade level. This is very important because if prior knowledge is missing or incomplete, then students will have a difficult time following the content sequence.

At the same time, teachers would have a clearer picture of how their standards-based curriculum aligns with the experienced curriculum in specific ways that effectively lead to acquisition of knowledge and development of skills. This can be accomplished by engaging school administrators in a collaborative approach to providing "leadership for learning" by listening, clarifying, presenting, problem solving, and negotiating (Glickman, 2002, p. 62).

POINTS TO PONDER . . .

The curricular problem faced by Lida stems from a lack of consistency related to the set of prior knowledge and skills that students should be able to demonstrate as they move up from one grade level to the next. How should teachers within the same school tackle the task of creating a curriculum revision team? Would you use Walker's deliberative approach? What procedural steps would you want to see in place as a result of this forming process? How could the team work best with other teachers within the school?

Walker's deliberative approach to curriculum planning relies on the process of interacting among different participants based on a variety of information sources designed to support the development of a new curriculum.

By the same token, what communication and dissemination tools should the team use to involve teachers and curriculum director(s) in the district? What kinds of evidence of student learning should the curriculum revision team take into account? Who should be responsible for what task?

QUESTIONS FOR ADMINISTRATORS

How would you increase accountability of student learning beyond the standardized test? How would you encourage communication among faculty members so that the curriculum time frame is effectively implemented while ensuring quality teaching and learning?

IN-CLASS ACTIVITY

Form interdisciplinary groups in your class so that you have at least one math teacher in each group. In collaborative fashion, generate a range of *instructional strategies designed to motivate students* to learn as part of a remedial class that would benefit students lacking prior knowledge and skills (at a grade level of your choice). As an extension of this activity, you could also brainstorm ideas related to developmentally appropriate diagnostic/formative assessment tools that could be used to inform instruction based on content standards that you are familiar with.

REFERENCES

Eisner, E. W. (1979). *The educational imagination.* Upper Saddle River, NJ: Merrill/ Prentice Hall.

Glickman, C. D. (2002). *Leadership for learning: How to help teachers succeed.* Alexandria, VA: Association for Supervision and Curriculum Development.

Stiggins, R. J., Arter, J. A., Chappuis, J., & Chappuis, S. (2006). *Classroom assessment for student learning: Doing it right—using it well.* Portland, OR: Educational Testing Service.

Taba, H. (1962). *Curriculum development: Theory and practice.* New York: Harcourt, Brace.

SUGGESTED READINGS

Earl, L. M. (2003). *Assessment as learning: Using classroom assessment to maximize student learning.* Thousand Oaks, CA: Corwin.

Posner, G. J., & Rudnitsky, A. N. (2006). *Course design: A guide to curriculum development for teachers* (7th ed.). Boston: Pearson.

Stiggins, R. (2008). *An introduction to student-involved assessment for learning* (5th ed.). Upper Saddle River, NJ: Pearson.

Tomlinson, C. A., & McTighe, J. (2006). *Integrating differentiated instruction and understanding by design.* Alexandria, VA: Association for Supervision and Curriculum Development.

Walker, D. F. (2003). *Fundamentals of curriculum* (2nd ed.). Mahwah, NJ: Lawrence Erlbaum.

Prevention Programs as Means to Teach Social Skills in Elementary School

Prereading Focus Points: Observing student behaviors in a variety of school settings (such as the hallways, the classrooms, or the playground) reveals certain differences. In some cases, positive behaviors are reinforced by a curricular focus on expected social skills. In other cases, students move from one classroom to the next with little awareness of set rules that are supposed to guide their behavior.

Level: Elementary

Content Area: N/A

Setting: Suburban

Spotlight on . . .
a) Social skills;
b) Hidden curriculum; and
c) Special education.

Key Terms: Hidden curriculum; D.A.R.E. (Drug Abuse Resistance Education)

BACKGROUND INFORMATION ABOUT THE TEACHER

Tracey is currently a substitute teacher for a large suburban school district, which supports three surrounding communities. The population of these communities is mainly Caucasian but also includes families of Hispanic, African American, Eastern European, and Arab descent. These communities are typically of a middle-class income level with a mix of white- and blue-collar workers. There are some areas that support lower-income residents with government-subsidized housing. As a result, students come from a variety of income levels. The district supports approximately 13,000 students across 22 buildings, with a variety of programs including special education, gifted, English as a Second Language (ESL), vocational, and day care as well as extended day care.

Tracey has been working as a substitute teacher on and off for this district for approximately the last 4 years. The majority of her assignments for the district have been in the area of special needs for grades K–6, even though her current certification is elementary education for grades 1–8. She was given the opportunity to substitute in a special needs classroom and found that she enjoyed working with those children. She has worked in pull-out/inclusion as well as self-contained classrooms. The children she works with have been diagnosed with a wide range of learning, emotional, and physical disabilities, ranging from LD (learning disabled) to MH (multiple-handicap) and SED (severely emotionally disturbed), including children with autism. Her previous teaching experience was at a Catholic school located within a major metropolitan area, in addition to several substituting opportunities in different suburban districts.

BACKGROUND INFORMATION ABOUT THE CURRICULUM

The curriculum denotes a goal-directed, ends-means approach. Learning experiences are generally structured around a district-selected textbook with some text-provided and teacher-developed activities intended to help the students meet the set objectives and state standards. At the elementary level, district-selected programs include language arts, math, science, social studies, art, physical education, and music. Assessment methods include informal (i.e., observation and anecdotal) and formal (i.e., written exams and standardized tests). In the area of special needs, children diagnosed as mild to moderate (i.e., LD and resource rooms) use the same textbooks as regular education. Students in these categories are typically presented with the program at their current cognitive level. Goals are based on their Individualized Education Plans (IEPs) and state standards. Assessments are also both informal and formal but usually include a modified assessment, and students are provided with additional resources to assist them, such as mathematics multiplication matrices and oral reading of exams. Materials and resources for the moderate to severely handicapped children are sourced and presented by the individual classroom teacher. Reading programs are commonly used in these classrooms. These children are typically in self-contained classrooms and rarely participate in inclusive environments. Assessments are also both informal and formal, with goals based on the students' IEPs, with alternate assessments designed to evaluate some state-required standards.

PROBLEM

Oftentimes, children with special needs display inappropriate social behaviors and skills, including disrespect of peers and adults and anger management issues, and generally display low self-esteem. Some of these behaviors are, in part, due to a child's disability (i.e., autism, attention deficit hyperactivity disorder, or severe emotional disturbance) and are being treated medically. Tracey has had the opportunity to work in all the elementary buildings and has noticed varying degrees of these inappropriate social behaviors, not only in children with special needs but also in children in regular education classrooms. Teachers typically deal with these behaviors through classroom management and positive reinforcement programs. The most commonly used program is the "card flipping," based on a "three-strikes" policy with a final consequence involving detention, or office visit, and parental contact. Teachers deal with misbehaviors on an incidental basis and typically do not have full discussions or lessons regarding socially acceptable behaviors and consequences for inappropriate actions.

Tracey thinks of these actions as representative of a "hidden" curriculum, as there are no set guidelines to follow and teachers and/or grade levels are given free range to develop any type of classroom management program they find suitable. Consequently, there is a range of (re)enforcement styles and a degree of discussions going on from classroom to classroom and school to school.

> **Hidden curriculum** could be perceived as anything that students learn without any evidence of or requirement for it, according to the planned or intended school curriculum.

Generally, she has found the classroom management plans to be successful, particularly in the K–3 environments. The problem with these programs is that, oftentimes, there are no lengthy discussions of what is socially appropriate behavior, how others may feel as a result of the behavior, and how it may impact how students feel about themselves. Children are only given a consequence without a full understanding of alternative behaviors. There is no program in place to provoke discussions amongst students and generate ideas for alternative behaviors. While it's understood that much of these behaviors should be learned at an early age in the home environment, Tracey has found through observations and experiences in the classroom that this doesn't appear to be happening. Parents or guardians are not always able or willing to address this at home due to work schedules, overlapping family responsibilities, and so forth. Therefore, the assumption is that the school will address these needs.

PROBING QUESTIONS

1. How would you address the issue of making expected social skills part of the formal/planned curriculum?

2. How would you "reveal" the part of the "hidden curriculum" dealing with student behavior as a way to cultivate positive social skills?

PROPOSED SOLUTION

As Nel Noddings (2003) put it, "we will not achieve even that meager success unless our children believe that they themselves are cared for and learn to care for others" (p. 59). Tracey believes it is important for schools to address the social skills that are not only used in the classroom but also transferable to the home and community environment. Children need to learn respect and caring not only for others but also for themselves. This will allow schools to turn out better citizens who will build better communities.

D.A.R.E. (Drug Abuse Resistance Education) is a highly acclaimed program offered to schoolchildren from kindergarten to 12th grade, featuring police officers participating actively in classrooms to address coping effectively with issues such as peer pressure, gang activity, violence, and drug/substance abuse.

Tracey's proposed solution is based on the framework of the D.A.R.E. program recently used in her district. As part of the program, students in certain grade levels spent time each week discussing and engaging in activities meant to raise drug-prevention awareness. Tracey would like to see teachers allot time each week for a discussion of social skills based on which to provide extension/follow-up activities built into the planned curriculum (i.e., language arts and social studies) that would reinforce these skills.

In an attempt to formalize the proposed solution, teachers would also meet to collaborate on the identification of skills to be taught at their grade level. Once these skills were selected, a range of classroom-based activities and community-based extension assignments would be agreed upon. Each set of strategies would have to have a certain timeline in place, along with an outline of all the necessary resources. Upon completion of such an initial cycle of implementation, participating educators would disseminate the strategies for teaching these skills that worked well in their classrooms.

With proper administrative support and following the initial implementation of the proposed solution, individual teachers would form problem-solving teams engaged in action research projects focused specifically on the development of positive social skills and their transfer into the family/community environment. This is exactly where the D.A.R.E. program experts could come in to serve as consultants. Suggested ideas would be to read children's literature that presents social skills and related issues such as respect, caring, compassion, and/or self-esteem during story time or language arts, followed by discussions or role-playing activities to model unacceptable and acceptable behaviors. Teachers could also discuss culturally based behaviors and logical consequences based on the culture currently being studied or centered on the topic of citizenship as presented in social studies. As a result of these actions, students should be able to develop a social contract that could be used as a "blueprint to guide the management of classroom behavior" (Henson, 2001, p. 52).

Traditional as well as Web-based literature could be utilized to design tolerance-building activities. If teachers were given ownership, they would be able to determine the most appropriate time and activities that would be suitable to their classrooms and meet to discuss what worked and didn't work in their classrooms, modifying the curriculum as needed. This could be utilized in both regular and special needs self-contained classrooms to varying degrees at all grade levels.

Findings from the action research projects would be shared with the whole school community as a way to integrate the teaching of social skills into the planned curriculum. Peer-based action groups at both the classroom and school levels would assist teachers and administration in monitoring the progress made in this respect.

EXPECTED OUTCOMES

As shown by recent studies, only a "concerted effort of parents, schools, media, and government" (Oliva, 2009, p. 498) can lead to substantially and consistently positive results in dealing with substance abuse. With this in mind, the success of the proposed solution relies on a set of evidence that brings together classrooms, the whole school as an entity, and the larger community in a concerted effort, as follows:

- Improved classroom behavior;
- Reduced frequency of measures required to deal with moderate to severe student misbehavior;
- Greater awareness and understanding of the impact of behaviors and consequences for students and others;
- Increased collaboration between teachers and students in terms of both prevention and effectively solving behavior problems;
- Improved confidence and self-esteem;
- Improved relationships at home, at school, and in the community; and
- Increased teacher participation in districtwide efforts aimed at dealing with negative social skills demonstrated by students.

POINTS TO PONDER . . .

Tracey emphasizes the need to address the deficient social skills demonstrated by some special education students in a consistent, coherent, and replicable manner across all disciplines taught in her school. How would you transition from a successful prevention program (such as D.A.R.E.) to teacher-driven initiatives aimed at continuing the efforts to improve students' social skills? How would you set aside time for social skill–building activities in the existing planned curriculum? How would you involve the larger community in your efforts to develop positive social skills in your students?

QUESTIONS FOR ADMINISTRATORS

Given the fact that Tracey is a substitute teacher, how would you bring everyone in your school on board when it comes to integrating a focus on social skills into the planned curriculum? If you were to implement Tracey's proposal to use action research projects, how would you motivate as well as reward teachers to participate in them?

IN-CLASS ACTIVITY

Secure access to the following set of documents: (a) a schoolwide management plan, (b) one (or preferably more than one) classroom management plan, and (c) a scope-and-sequence chart or curriculum map. Based on all these, run a collaborative analysis of how each one of them aligns with the rest of them.

Identify specific areas of social skills that seem to be addressed in a coherent manner by all documents you have just analyzed. At the same time, list any divergent areas where social skills do not seem to translate into the formal/planned curriculum. Share your findings with the whole class and determine a preliminary plan of action based on which social skills could be taught effectively.

REFERENCES

Henson, K. T. (2001). *Curriculum planning: Integrating multiculturalism, constructivism, and education reform* (2nd ed.). Long Grove, IL: Waveland Press, Inc.

Noddings, N. (2003). Teaching themes of care. In A. C. Ornstein, L. S. Behar-Horenstein, & E. F. Pajak (Eds.), *Contemporary issues in curriculum* (3rd ed., pp. 59–65). Boston: Allyn & Bacon.

Oliva, P. F. (2009). *Developing the curriculum* (7th ed.). Boston: Allyn & Bacon.

SUGGESTED READINGS

Ginsberg, R. B. (2002, June). Board of Education of Independent School District No. 92 of Pottawatomie County, et al., Petitioners v. Lindsay Earls et al. In D. Evans (Ed.), *Taking sides: Clashing views on controversial issues in teaching and educational practice* (2nd ed., pp. 273–276). Dubuque, IA: McGraw-Hill/Dushkin.

Kohn, A. (2004, Fall). Safety from the inside out: Rethinking traditional approaches. In J. W. Noll (Ed.), *Taking sides: Clashing views on educational issues* (14th ed., pp. 318–325). Dubuque, IA: McGraw-Hill.

Model Me Kids. (n.d.). *Videos for modeling social skills for children with Asperger syndrome and autism.* Retrieved June 9, 2009, from http://www.modelmekids.com

Northeast Foundation for Children, Inc. (n.d.). *Responsive classroom web site.* Retrieved June 9, 2009, from http://www.responsiveclassroom.org

Ornstein, A. C., & Hunkins, F. P. (2004). *Curriculum: Foundations, principles, and issues* (4th ed.). Boston: Allyn & Bacon.

Sandbox Learning Educational Tools (for children with special needs). (n.d.). *Welcome to Sandbox Learning.* Retrieved June 9, 2009, from http://www.sandbox-learning.com

Shanker, A. (1995, May 15). Restoring the connection between behavior and consequences. In J. W. Noll (Ed.), *Taking sides: Clashing views on educational issues* (14th ed., pp. 308–317). Dubuque, IA: McGraw-Hill.

Thomas, C. (2002, June). Board of Education of Independent School District No. 92 of Pottawatomie County, et al., Petitioners v. Lindsay Earls et al. In D. Evans (Ed.), *Taking sides: Clashing views on controversial issues in teaching and educational practice* (2nd ed., pp. 268–272). Dubuque, IA: McGraw-Hill/Dushkin.

CASE 13

Educating the Community About a Needed Levy Increase

The Teacher as a Political Activist

Prereading Focus Points: Principals and superintendents look into their teaching ranks for potential leaders. In this case study, a teacher with apparent ambitions for leadership is asked to participate in designing a plan to ensure the passage of the next levy vote; the last one had failed, and she and her colleagues were set to feel the negative impact of decreased funding in a growing school and district. It's common knowledge that teachers are too often confronted with diminishing resources. All members of the school community are greatly impacted by the passing or rejection of a levy to increase property taxes that would, in turn, increase funding for schools. The teacher in this case study has shouldered a heavy burden.

Level: Districtwide

Content Area: N/A

Setting: Inner-ring suburban

Spotlight on . . .
   a) Engaging community; and
   b) Role of teacher beyond the classroom.

Key Terms: Inner-ring suburb; mill; levy

BACKGROUND INFORMATION ABOUT THE TEACHER

Amy has been a high school social studies teacher for the past 5 years. Prior to this teaching position she taught middle school social studies for 4 years. Amy also worked in a criminal defense law firm for 1 year preceding her teaching career and had every intention of attending law school the following year. She received her bachelor's degree in non-Western history in an attempt to prepare herself for law school, where the focus of her studies would be on immigration law.

An **inner-ring suburb** refers to a city located adjacent to a much larger, highly urbanized city. It often has the same characteristics as the larger city including similar socioeconomic status of its inhabitants. An outer-ring and/or exurb, by contrast, is usually a wealthier, "bedroom" community farther away from the central city.

Amy was approached during the end of her first year clerking to teach at an inner-city Roman Catholic school. This opportunity seemed a viable way for her to support herself during law school. As it turned out, she enjoyed teaching more than working at the law firm and decided to pursue a teaching certification from a local private university. Amy was afforded the opportunity to teach under administrators who helped shape her management and instructional methods. She has taught primarily in inner-city schools in both private and public arenas, and subsequently, her primary concern and focus in education has become the impact of funding on student performance and district report cards. This has led her to seek her master's degree in school administration and to choose to focus her career on better understanding the complex nature of school finance and funding resources.

A **mill** is one one-thousandth of a dollar and is used in reference to the property tax rate percentage that is to be assessed for individual homeowners. Typically one half of a school district's income is derived from property taxes, and a levy needs to be accepted by voters in order to increase the mills assessed. Without a successful **levy** (a change in mills usually requiring a public vote) campaign, schools can be faced with the cutting of programs and even layoffs.

Amy has been afforded the opportunity to participate in a levy campaign for the following year, a huge responsibility for anyone but a great opportunity for someone with Amy's ambition and passion. Designing and implementing a successful campaign has been a tremendous asset to her knowledge base on school finance and the interwoven nature of the politics of education.

BACKGROUND INFORMATION ABOUT THE SCHOOL AND ITS COMMUNITY

Adams is a small community of 11,700 residents and is an inner-ring suburb of a large Midwestern city. The homes in Adams cover an area of 4.5 miles and primarily consist of brick bungalows or ranch-style homes built 30 years ago. There are a small number of new-construction homes that are colonial and a number of apartment buildings, which appeal to the transient population of this inner-ring suburb. Adams has a thriving industrial and retail base, which allows taxes to remain relatively low at 62.9 mills. The houses in Adams are generally appraised consistently lower than the selling prices. Shopping and other needed amenities are prevalent, and most retailers, mostly large chains, are easily accessible.

Adams High School, where Amy currently teaches, has a graduating class of 89 students and a total population 505 high school students. Although small for a high school, it is growing dramatically. The community is tightly knit, and a large portion of the school's students have parents who also attended the Adams city schools. Until recently, Adams was not a typical inner-ring suburb in that its population did not resemble that of its larger neighbor. That began to change about 5 years ago when a highly transient population emerged, one that is as diverse racially and socioeconomically as the large city just to the north of Adams. This new population has created a social tension between the "old" and "new" residents. The district spends $7,689 per student each year and has a 98% graduation rate, and 76% of students attend college. The community strongly supports retired adults who receive many benefits from the city such as snow removal, grass cutting, medical screenings, and transportation.

PROBLEM

In order to pay for an operating deficit, the city of Adams needs additional funds. State funding has been frozen, and operating income has been lost due to delinquent taxes, foreclosures, and bankruptcies. Adams is situated in the heart of the "Rustbelt" where manufacturing jobs have all but disappeared, leaving cities and some states in dire straits. Seven years ago an emergency 3-year 5-mill levy was passed to pay for debt accrued by the district during a fiscal emergency due to the dismal economic downturn of the past several years.

Another 7.9-mill levy was up earlier this year—and failed; the Adams Board of Education has made the necessary cuts to balance the budget. A new 6.6-mill levy will be on the ballot this year, and the new levy amount reflects the cuts that were approved during the most recent Board of Education meeting. The 6.6-mill levy is designed to simply maintain the current functions of the district after the reductions have been made. This new amount does not reinstate any programs or staffing. It is designed not to pay for new programs or stave off future budget cuts but simply to maintain what the district has. The 5-year plan of the district shows a slow progression of the reinstatement of needed programs and staffing in a growing school district.

PROBING QUESTION

1. How will Amy and her district create an effective communication plan in the community to stress the importance of a successful levy, especially for those who do not have children attending school (retired community members, childless couples, families with children attending private institutions)?

ACTUAL SOLUTION

First, Amy and her colleagues determined that they must get organized and developed a levy committee directly responsible for the communication of levy information. This committee included citizens and staff and served as an advisory council in the decision-making process. Next, they held "District Dialogues" that resembled public roundtable meetings. The superintendent of schools routinely scheduled meetings immediately following a defeated levy. These meetings now became the District Dialogues with the community, especially targeting those without children in Adams city schools.

The District Dialogues were used as a way to formulate data and determine recommendations for the budget based on public opinion. They created a sense of importance, and the community members began to feel that their ideas and beliefs were heard; some were even utilized.

Community members stated during the "District Dialogues" that they felt out of the loop and therefore literature and information should be sent into the community in the form of literature drops, mailings, local newspapers, public access television, the Internet, and word of mouth. At these District Dialogues accusations from the public and misinformation held and believed by the public were addressed. In addition, the superintendent responded to these accusations as well as to what he believed to be rumors and misinformation in the form of letters to the editor and paid advertisements in the local newspaper. He also had campaign flyers distributed and e-mailed residents who had supplied the district with their addresses.

In addition to the District Dialogues, neighborhood meetings were held in the homes of volunteers and attended by all residents to address issues regarding the upcoming levy. These were conducted in a personal and informal manner. A Web page was launched that had a question-and-answer format and allowed the community to interact with the decision makers.

In the past, the outcomes of both a "yes" and a "no" vote on the levy were not clearly defined and communicated. The levy committee planned a public advance notice list of the superintendent's recommended budget cuts if the next one were to fail. Additionally, the levy committee was represented at all community functions and open dialogues. Finally, the levy committee sent volunteers to canvass the community to speak with residents about the importance of the levy and listen to their concerns.

During all dialogue with the public, the importance of the correlation between property values and the public school system was stressed. Data were provided about the district's expenses in the form of charts that showed annual, monthly, and weekly operating expenses—how the district's tax money was being spent and was to be spent if the levy passed.

OBSERVED OUTCOMES

This strategic plan was designed to create a successful levy. Despite the outcome of the levy, the process initiated by the levy committee and the superintendent may have created a more educated community on matters regarding their schools. These include issues related to school funding on the state, local, and federal levels. A better understanding may now exist about education and the correlation between the schools and property values and the drastic cuts that were made as a result of the last unsuccessful levy. Projected cuts for the following school year were clearly stated, and communication was opened up to dispel all misconceptions and misinformation about the direction of the district.

Amy took on a great responsibility as a teacher—a responsibility that may seem above and beyond her role as a teacher in the Adams School District. She did this willingly as she has a passion for increasing funds to better serve the schools and her students.

POINTS TO PONDER . . .

Despite her passion, Amy was a bit reluctant to become so involved in the levy campaign. She would be in a high-profile position at her school and in her community, and tax levies are often politically controversial. As a teacher, how comfortable would you feel becoming so involved in such a "hot" issue? Would you feel comfortable saying "no" to upper administration? Should teachers be asked by administration to participate in what could be considered a political activity? If you *did* feel comfortable participating in the act of communicating with the public, would it make a difference if you lived in the community or outside? Would it make a difference to the community—the voters? How would your participation, or lack thereof, affect your standing with your colleagues? With your students? How much should students be involved in a campaign to increase a property tax levy? What is the teacher's classroom role in these campaigns, especially those that are so well advertised in the community?

QUESTIONS FOR ADMINISTRATORS

How comfortable would you be having your teachers become politically active in the community, even when that activity is focused on improving the conditions of the schools? What might be the positive results? Negative results? What if the activity were not directly linked to the schools? Do you feel that it is your role as a school-based administrator to become politically active in your community in order to improve the schools? Would it make a difference if you were a district-level administrator?

IN-CLASS ACTIVITY

With two or three classmates, discuss your answers to the above questions. Individually, but in collaboration with your peers, develop a "manifesto" stating how you will support your students, your school, your school district, and the community. This should be no more than one to two pages in length and will start out "As an engaged teacher, I will . . ."

SUGGESTED READINGS

Crowther, F., Ferguson, M., & Hann, L. (2009). *Developing teacher leaders: How teacher leadership enhances school success* (2nd ed.). Thousand Oaks, CA: Corwin.

Kenyon, D. A. (2007). *The property tax–school funding dilemma* (Policy Focus Report). Abstract retrieved August 14, 2008, from http://www.lincolninst.edu/pubs/pubdetail .aspx?pubid=1308

Reeves, D. B. (2008). *Reframing teacher leadership to improve your school*. Alexandria, VA: Association for Supervision and Curriculum Development.

The Mandated Curriculum Meeting the Needs of Teachers and Their Favored Practices

Prereading Focus Points: Teachers experience frustration when a curriculum, even a high-quality curriculum, is forced upon them by well-intentioned administrators. Here we examine a teacher's frustration as well as the ideas she develops to work with mandates so they can meet her individual needs and allow her to do what she knows is in the best interests of her students.

Level: Elementary

Content Area: Language arts

Setting: Suburban

Spotlight on . . .

    a) Mandated curriculum;
    b) Teacher autonomy; and
    c) Accountability.

Key Terms: Favored practices; looping; teacher autonomy

BACKGROUND INFORMATION ABOUT THE TEACHER

Brandie has been teaching in some capacity for 8 years. She began as a substitute working in eight districts in the Midwest (grades K–8, all subjects) and eventually became a Title I tutor at a facility that housed children with behavioral disorders. There, she worked for 2 years with neglected and delinquent minors who were unable to attend mainstream, public schooling. From there, Brandie ventured out to a public middle school and spent 2 years teaching eighth-grade reading. Her adventurous spirit, as she likes to say, took her to a sixth-grade classroom at a public elementary school in the Spanish Harlem section of New York City. She explains that 1 year there was more than enough—Brandie is now at a public middle school back in the Midwest teaching seventh-grade language arts (with one world history class) and, for the most part, is loving it. This is also her first year as the Reading Curriculum Leader at her school.

Brandie's curiosity and need for finances led her to explore Quantum Learning Network's (QLN's) SuperCamp last summer. The training she received at the 10-day academic camp helped shape the teacher that Brandie is today. She has always tried to be creative and have fun with her lessons. QLN, according to Brandie, taught her various memory techniques to use with her students as well as strategies to "captivate their brains" and keep them attentive. Using music in the classroom for "state changes" as well as for increasing the effectiveness of the learning environment is just one example.

> We've all heard of "best practice" or what research and experience tell us is effective in our teaching. The title of this case study uses the phrase **"favored practice"** to refer to what we are most comfortable using even if it does or does not improve learning in our classroom.

Brandie works on a three-person team at a middle school (grades 6–8) of about 1,500 students. Her team is small; therefore, her class size averages 24 students. Brandie's classroom offers a colorful, welcoming environment with a full wall of windows that look out to a courtyard. She also has 10 computers for student use. The desks are set up in what she calls "runway" style so that each student can see the others and Brandie can see them all as well. She varies her instruction within the 55-minute class and throughout the week. The students work individually, in ever-changing small groups, and as a whole class.

BACKGROUND INFORMATION ABOUT THE CURRICULUM

Brandie's school district aims to teach her state's published standards and benchmarks. She and her colleagues are also told to incorporate district goals, such as thinking globally and using technology. The district's curriculum director introduced middle school language arts teachers to a different approach for the teaching of reading and writing toward the end of the last school year: Nancie Atwell's (1998) reading/writing workshop.

Atwell's workshop is not a new concept; she has been teaching in this way, conducting seminars, and writing books on this topic since 1987. The basis of the idea is to create an environment that, according to Atwell (1998, p. 4), "invites and supports writing and reading so that when my students arrive they'll find what they need to begin to act as writers and readers: time, materials and texts, space, and ways for them, and for me, to monitor our activity, organize our work, and think about what writers and readers in a workshop might do."

The students read self-selected books from a classroom library and answer weekly journal prompts. Students' journal entries are written in the form of a letter to the teacher and are a reflection of their readings. The teacher then responds to each entry and offers feedback, thoughts, answers, and questions. This journal becomes a one-on-one, private conversation between teacher and student.

During the silent reading time, the students may also be working on a type of writing to which they have been previously introduced, such as expository. The students submit copies to the teacher for publication. Spelling words and mechanics are individualized based on student writing level of ability. Poetry plays a huge role in the first few weeks as the children create their "heart map" and discover their "writing territories." They are required to publish a certain number of works per term, and the opportunity for sharing is frequent.

Brandie has just begun to implement only the reading portion in this last quarter of school. Currently, the average day in her classroom starts out with reading workshop for 15–20 minutes depending on the class level. The remaining class time is dedicated to a major writing assignment, a mini lesson, and independent writing and/or conferencing time.

PROBLEM

Brandie considers herself to be open when it comes to trying new things. When she was first introduced to the reading/writing workshop approach, Brandie immediately saw problems with it. There were time issues as well as implementation and content concerns. She also felt the mandate to change to this model ("strong suggestion," as it was worded) interfered with her own ideologies about teaching.

In Brandie's school, teachers and students are on a schedule that allots 55 minutes per class period. The students have four academic courses and two electives, such as band or art. One of the academics is a combined reading and writing course: language arts. In their state, seventh graders are tested in reading, writing, and mathematics. This means that, as a language arts teacher, Brandie has 55 minutes a day to prepare students for two state tests, the same

Following a group of students for 2 or more years is often referred to as **"looping"** or "continuity of caring."

amount of time teachers in other subject areas have to prepare for one. This creates the time constraint that concerned her about the workshop method. Nancie Atwell's school in Boothbay Harbor, Maine, is on a block schedule format. This means teachers there have somewhere around an hour and 30 minutes per day to conduct a workshop. And because Brandie has her students in sixth, seventh, and eighth grades, she also thought the students might get bored with this way of learning after 3 straight years of it!

Brandie was immediately concerned with the workload involved with this type of teaching strategy as it would cause her to completely change the way she has always taught. The district's curriculum director, who had taught this way in his previous position, spoke frequently of the enormous amount of grading and preparation time spent outside of the classroom. Brandie's personal time is something that she tries to protect, trying to get most of her work done at school to allow her evenings to be free for family and friends. This new model would not allow for that. Not only did the classroom need to be completely reworked, but each teacher was given four Atwell books to read. The objective was for the language arts teachers to be able to understand and implement her strategies effectively.

What disturbed Brandie the most about this way of teaching was its ability to prepare her students for the state achievement tests. As previously mentioned, her state tests seventh graders on both reading and writing skills. There are very specific skills that the students need to understand and perform to pass this test. Parts of speech, vocabulary, essay writing, and tracking down information from a reading selection are only a few. Brandie felt that the reading/writing workshop did not address all the content standards. She, like most educators in this era of accountability, constantly worries about her students passing high-stakes tests. Brandie and many of her colleagues feel students need direct instruction and practice with these skills in order to pass these tests.

Brandie's final concern with the reading/writing workshop is that it was pushed on her and her colleagues from above. The curriculum director was enthusiastic and confident that every language arts teacher in the district would

Teacher autonomy is a hot topic in the age of accountability. Do teachers have academic freedom when they are mandated to teach a certain curriculum?

join the reading and writing workshop bandwagon. Brandie likes the way she teaches and doesn't see any major concerns with the way she conducts her classroom and lessons. Her school's seventh graders produced an 85% passage rate on the writing test last year and came close to passing reading. Brandie says, "If it ain't broke, why fix it?"

PROBING QUESTIONS

1. Is there room in the reading/writing approach for individuality? Could teachers conduct a mandated teaching and learning approach while keeping their own ideologies in place?

2. Should the workshop model be a gradual implementation? Would it be better for students to be introduced to it in sixth grade and eventually go full force in eighth?

PROPOSED SOLUTION

Resolving these problems would have to address *teacher freedom* and *gradual implementation*. In addition to her concern that the reading and writing workshop method was mandated from above, Brandie also has problems with this being too tedious to be effective, all year, every year.

Brandie has only been teaching for 8 years, but she already has teaching systems she created, borrowed, or changed with which she is very happy. She can only imagine what it would be like for a veteran teacher of 20 to 30 years. She understands how teachers can be set in their ways, but they know what does and what does not work for them and their students. With this in mind, Brandie proposes that teachers have the freedom to implement the reading/writing workshop in a way that fits their own teaching styles and ideologies—not what was mandated by her curriculum director.

The writing workshop curriculum has a lot to it. There are many lessons and strategies that Atwell suggests must all be used. Brandie has taught a few of the writing lessons and found them quite beneficial. There are others, however, that she feels are not. She picked the lessons that best suited her needs as well as her students'. She firmly believes that if you are not passionate about what and how you are teaching, then the knowledge is not as easily obtained by your students. Therefore, according to Brandie, teachers should be able to implement the reading/writing workshop in a way that keeps them passionate; they need to be permitted to make it their own! This freedom would also eliminate the time concerns that were described above.

One day after school, two eighth graders (whom Brandie taught the previous year, prior to the implementation of looping) stopped by her classroom. Their current teacher has been using the workshop method in full force since the beginning of the school year. Brandie decided to probe them for information and opinions. Their answers did not surprise her: They liked the model but found it "boring after a while." To eliminate the chances of this model becoming stale to both the teacher and students, she decided that the reading/writing workshop should be a gradual implementation that develops over the course of 3 years (sixth through eighth grade) rather than be foisted upon all grades at once.

If the students are already bored with this curriculum after 8 months, Brandi reasoned, how are they going to feel after 30? With gradual implementation, they can learn the basics of grammar and mechanics in sixth grade, add to them in seventh, and practice the full writing workshop model in eighth.

According to Brandie, sixth graders are already overwhelmed with lockers, changing classes, and the other changes that come from moving from an elementary to a middle school. The reading/writing workshop at the start of sixth grade, to her, would be too much stress. She proposes that they learn the basics at least three fourths of the way through the year. The teachers, with their own ideologies in place, can conduct a mini workshop with fewer requirements and less emphasis on the writing workshop's guidelines. In seventh grade, the students would now be familiar with the model but not fully practicing it. The seventh-grade teachers would implement parts of the curriculum during the part of the year that they chose. By eighth grade, the workshop approach would be in full swing for most of the year.

EXPECTED OUTCOMES

Brandie concedes that Nancie Atwell's writing workshop shows a lot of promise and could very well be a wonderful curriculum. Individuality of teachers and students can be encouraged through this method, but it also needs to be recognized from the start. The solutions she has proposed will help make this method reach its full potential.

According to Brandie, by giving the teachers the much needed permission to be unique, you are ultimately being supportive rather than forceful. When it came to giving support for this workshop, the curriculum director said he only wanted to "water the flowers." She and some of her colleagues did not feel that way. The feeling was more of an all-or-nothing mandate. Brandie feels he should have said, "Here are the basics of the workshop method; make it your own." The outcome of this would have been a heightened interest in the curriculum from the teachers and a welcomed challenge.

Furthermore, Brandie is sure that the outcome of the gradual introduction of the reading/writing workshop would be phenomenal in comparison to a full 3-year practice. The sixth graders would have the first three quarters of the year to get used to middle school while still learning the state standards. Fourth quarter is already a relaxed 9 weeks, so introducing the workshop at this time would be ideal. Students and teachers would view this as more of an end-of-the-year activity than a pressured unit of study. The seventh graders would begin their year as normal, reading and writing to learn the state standards. About halfway through the year, the reintroduction to the workshop would occur. The outcome would be low stress because it was that way in sixth grade. As time went on and more parts were put into place, the students would gain mastery of skills and understand the methods with ease. Once in eighth grade, the reading/writing workshop would be full speed ahead. Students would still have a relaxed attitude toward the curriculum. They would have come far with a comprehension of the system itself and would have drastically increased their reading levels.

These proposed solutions, Brandie posits, create a friendly atmosphere for new staff and students. By easing into the curriculum and giving choices to the teachers, there is a lot less pressure on learning. New staff will still have choices as to how they run their classroom, and new students will feel comfortable in the environment that has been created. The reading and writing workshop is a well-planned but strict curriculum that can be effective if altered to meet the needs of individual teachers and students. With minor adjustments in implementation and more freedom in planning, it can make any child an effective reader and writer.

POINTS TO PONDER . . .

The curriculum described has been implemented successfully by language arts teachers around the country (including one of this book's editors). In this light, can "one size fit all"? That is, can one curriculum and instruction model meet the needs and fit the styles of all teachers in a district? In a school? If so, how? If not, why? How important is it to stick to a published curriculum? Will straying from it cause you to lose its effectiveness? How much authority should administrators have on *what* you teach—the curriculum? How much authority should they have on *how* you teach? How would you feel about being forced to follow a mandated curriculum? What is your opinion about all teachers being held accountable to teaching to statewide standards? To statewide student tests?

QUESTIONS FOR ADMINISTRATORS

Some of the questions posed above could be easily aimed at you, as follows: How much authority should administrators have on what teachers teach and how they teach? If you were required by your school board or superintendent to use a mandated curriculum at your school or in your district, how would you convince *all* teachers to do so? How would you combat teacher resistance? Would you resist? If so, what might be the consequences? How would you explain your position to your superiors in the district?

IN-CLASS ACTIVITY

Find a classmate who is teaching a subject or a level similar to yours. Together, write a letter to the editor of your local newspaper stating your professional opinion as a teacher regarding the mandates that come from federal, state, and local authorities and their impact on your practice. This should be limited to 300 words or less.

REFERENCE

Atwell, N. (1998). *In the middle: New understanding about writing, reading, and learning (workshop series)*. Portsmouth, NH: Boyton/Cook.

SUGGESTED READINGS

Cuban, L. (2001). *How can I fix it? Finding solutions and managing dilemmas: An educator's road map*. New York: Teachers College Press.

Reeves, D. B. (2002). *Making standards work: How to implement standards-based assessments in the classroom, school, and district* (3rd ed., paperback). Denver, CO: Advanced Learning Centers.

Reeves, D. B. (2004). *Accountability for learning: How teachers and school leaders can take charge*. Alexandria, VA: Association for Supervision and Curriculum Development.

Balancing Data-Driven Decision Making and Shifting Paradigms in a New Elementary Math Curriculum

Prereading Focus Points: An elementary teacher is involved in a districtwide enactment of a new mathematics program purchased in an attempt to meet the state standards, which test scores indicated were not being met. The identified standards focus on higher-order learning, such as reasoning and problem-solving skills. The author describes the process of curriculum implementation, including challenges, outcomes, and the impact on her as an elementary school teacher. One specific area of interest is constructivism, as the school district hinted that it would need to be embraced if the standards were to be met and the new program were to be implemented effectively.

Level: Elementary

Content Area: Mathematics

Setting: Urban/suburban

Spotlight on . . .

    a) Implementation of districtwide curriculum; and
    b) Accountability requirements.

Key Terms: Highly Qualified Teacher (HQT); constructivism

BACKGROUND INFORMATION ABOUT THE TEACHER

Christy is an elementary teacher who served on the districtwide "Mathematics Teacher Leadership Team." She's taught at Oxford Elementary School for 8 years in various roles, including reading specialist, kindergarten teacher, and second-grade teacher.

"Highly Qualified Teacher" (HQT) represents the designation classroom practitioners receive based on specific criteria outlined by the No Child Left Behind Act.

Christy's building is a K–5 public school located in the Osmond Heights City School District. Oxford is situated within an ethnically, culturally, and economically diverse school district of 6,500 students that borders a large, economically challenged city. The State Department of Education classifies the Osmond Heights City School District as "urban" based on its high percentage of students receiving free and reduced-price meals as well as its racially diverse student population. Oxford Elementary School serves 375 students—approximately 90% are minorities. Economically disadvantaged students comprise about 60% of the student population, and students with disabilities make up nearly 13% of the population. The entire teaching faculty meets the federally mandated "Highly Qualified Teacher" requirements, and over 50% of the teaching staff holds at least a master's degree.

BACKGROUND INFORMATION ABOUT THE CURRICULUM

In the past, teachers at Oxford taught mathematics, and students learned mathematics in much the same way as they did when the school's doors first opened in the mid-1900s. As times changed, the curriculum materials looked more sophisticated and the workbooks were more colorful, but the same teaching and learning methods prevailed.

Most teachers taught mathematics using "traditional" methods of instruction, thus mimicking the ways they had learned mathematics themselves. Lessons typically followed the same four steps, with the second one consuming most of the instructional time:

1. A brief review of homework assignments and conceptual material covered in class the previous class period

2. Teacher-directed instruction about a new mathematical concept or skill

3. Independent practice time for students, while teacher circulates to assist struggling students

4. A brief explanation of new homework assignments following the current lesson

PROBLEM

Teachers and students seemed quite comfortable with the curriculum model being used, but it wasn't "adding up" to success for the students. The principal and teachers were especially troubled when the No Child Left Behind legislation made them more accountable for student achievement. After analyzing mathematics proficiency data from fourth-grade students (see Table 15.1), the entire school community grew concerned.

Constructivism is a way of thinking about how learning takes place. Advocates of this view believe that all of what one learns is done so through the lens of his or her experiences. In other words, none of us is an "empty vessel" into which a teacher can pour knowledge. We must understand all content by negotiating it with what we already know.

Table 15.1   Oxford's Fourth-Grade Test Results on the "State Mathematics Proficiency Test"

School Year	Proficiency Percentage
2000–2001	44.2%
2001–2002	52.3%
2002–2003	43.8%
2003–2004	38.4%

Clearly, the scores on standardized and state-mandated mathematics tests did not meet the expectations. After analyzing these data and state standards for mathematics, district curriculum specialists determined that students needed more than computation skills. Educators needed to help students gain deeper conceptual understandings of mathematics.

PROBING QUESTIONS

1. How can teachers and administrators align their efforts to meet both the needs of their students and the current accountability requirements with districtwide plans?

2. What resources are needed to implement curriculum change based on data-driven decision making?

ACTUAL SOLUTION

To support both teachers and students, the district purchased a new, research-based mathematics series. *Everyday Mathematics,* adopted in 2003, provided more than new curriculum materials. The district recognized that it was committing to implementing a new curricular model, which ultimately required a paradigm shift from traditional to constructivist, student-centered teaching strategies. The main rationale that prompted the change derived from the need to encourage learners to "construct" their knowledge by interacting with others and their environment. This type of active learning promotes the growth of students' mathematical reasoning and problem-solving skills. In a constructivist classroom, the emphasis is on the process of how one arrives at a particular answer, rather than the product of finding the one correct solution (Doyle, 1990a).

In its action plan for implementation, the district acknowledged that teachers would need support in learning how to effectively use the new materials in their classrooms. This involved ongoing teacher professional development, as well as training "teacher leaders" at each building. During the 2003–2004 implementation year, teachers attended in-services every other month. An *Everyday Math* consultant worked with the teachers; she also conducted some follow-up sessions at each elementary building. For example, the math consultant visited Oxford and taught a model lesson in a first-grade classroom; teachers from other primary classrooms were given release time to observe. Such authentic learning experiences gave teachers a firsthand glimpse of constructivist math teaching in action.

District elementary principals selected two teachers from each school to serve on the "Mathematics Teacher Leadership Team." Teacher Leaders had additional in-service days throughout 2003–2004 and 2004–2005; the goal was for them to take on the role of "math consultant" in their buildings. At Oxford, the math leaders shared promising practices at each monthly staff meeting. Peer coaching and modeling were also part of the process. Additionally, the "Mathematics Teacher Leadership Team" developed curriculum maps for implementation at the elementary buildings. Within 2 years of adopting the program, the district no longer needed to pay for the services of the math consultants. The district had cultivated its own in-house math "experts" by providing select educators with additional professional development and training opportunities.

School leaders did not expect a magical transformation in outcomes overnight. However, with all of the money and resources expended for professional development, they did expect to see gradual changes in teaching practices. Principals were trained by the math consultant on how to observe in elementary mathematics classrooms. The math consultant gave administrators detailed checklists that outlined what to look for during classroom observations. Prior to coming into classrooms, the Oxford principal shared these checklist forms with her teaching staff so everyone was aware of the expectations.

OBSERVED OUTCOMES

Curriculum leaders at the district level expected to see gradual improvements with student achievement outcomes—and they got them. The State Department of Education measures the effectiveness of its schools through achievement test results. Therefore, at Oxford the goal was to meet or exceed the state requirement of having 75% or more students at or above the "proficient" level on the Mathematics Achievement Test. While there were no substantial gains during the implementation year, by the following academic year, the fourth-grade State Mathematics Proficiency Test scores jumped from 38.4% proficient (in 2003–2004) to 75% proficient (in 2004–2005).

Oxford's principal and teachers worked collaboratively to closely monitor student achievement data. An emphasis was placed on mathematics outcomes in third, fourth, and fifth grades, since students at those levels take achievement tests. By the 2005–2006 academic year, Oxford Elementary School was celebrating successful gains on the Mathematics Achievement Tests (see Table 15.2). Nevertheless, these results suggested that more intensive work was needed in the upper-intermediate grade levels. By 2006–2007, the district made plans to hire a

Table 15.2 Oxford's Test Results on the "State Mathematics Proficiency Test" in 2005–2006

Grade Level	Proficiency Percentage
Third	79.3%
Fourth	80.0%
Fifth	68.3%

part-time Mathematics Instructional Coach at Oxford for the following school year. The role of the math coach would be to assist teachers in continuing to strengthen their mathematics teaching and to ultimately impact student achievement in mathematics.

By the conclusion of 2007–2008, the goal was to have 85% or more students proficient in mathematics at all achievement test grade levels, thus exceeding the minimum state requirement by 10 or more percentage points.

Will these students and teachers live "happily ever after"? Will the school's test scores continue to show improvement? That remains to be seen. Clearly, these educators are attempting to create meaningful mathematical curricular changes. Ultimately, their goal is to make it all "add up" to mathematical success for *all* students!

POINTS TO PONDER . . .

What would be your reaction to a district-mandated planned/designed curriculum (textbook) for your classroom? As a teacher at this particular school, what evidence would you need to see to be convinced that this program is effective? What other tools and strategies would you recommend to supplement the analysis of the assessed curriculum focused on standardized testing data? In other words, what else can Christy do to document student growth and progress? Given the standards-based curriculum mandated by the district, what role do you think society and/or the individual could play in sustaining the effective implementation of the new elementary math curriculum?

QUESTIONS FOR ADMINISTRATORS

How do you think a school and/or district can ensure that all teachers are shifting their teaching practices toward the new teaching approach? What should a principal do if some teachers are resistant to change? What kinds of professional development opportunities would be most effective for the teachers described in the case study?

At a Parent-Teacher Association meeting, a group of parents express their disappointment with the school's new math program. Some of the teaching methods and algorithms are unfamiliar to the parents, so they are not able to assist their children with the nightly homework assignments. With a classmate, discuss how you would respond to these parents. Once you have your responses written, your instructor will ask two students to role-play teachers attending this meeting. These students will respond to the parents while the rest of the class plays the role of parents. Another student will play the role of the principal and/or district curriculum administrator.

REFERENCE

Doyle, W. (1990a). Classroom knowledge as a foundation for learning. *Teachers College Record, 91*(3), 347–360.

SUGGESTED READINGS

Doyle, W. (1990b). Themes in teacher education research. In W. R. Houston (Ed.), *Handbook of research on teacher education* (pp. 3–23). New York: Macmillan.

National Research Council. (2000). *How people learn: Brain, mind, experience, and school*. Washington, DC: National Academy Press.

Case 16

Professional Development That Works, Please!

Prereading Focus Points: A teacher recently hired as a district-level supervisor for professional development runs into some problems related to the parameters of her work. A group of educators representing each school is empowered to make decisions about districtwide professional development, ostensibly based on the needs of each school. Due to budget constraints, this diverse school district must make do with only one professional development day each year, making the committee's and the supervisor's job very difficult as the needs of each school and its students greatly differ.

Level: District

Content Area: All

Setting: Urban/suburban

Spotlight on . . . Districtwide professional development

Key Term: Professional development

BACKGROUND INFORMATION ABOUT THE TEACHER

Molly has just been hired as the secondary curriculum director for a large public school district. The district is composed of 3,000 students and 200 certified and noncertified staff. Seventy percent of the students are African American, and the other 30% are White. As part of her job, Molly is responsible for heading the professional development committee. This committee's sole charge is to plan and implement a one-day professional development seminar for the entire district. It is important to include the needs of all certified staff (K–12). The committee is composed of two to three teachers from each building in the district and two administrators. They serve as the voices for the entire district at the building level, taking input from the teachers in their building and bringing it back to the committee.

BACKGROUND INFORMATION ABOUT THE CURRICULUM

Molly understands that the two most challenging aspects of this position are working with the small budget of $1,000 and meeting the needs of all teachers. The budget causes many obstacles. In addition, it's common knowledge in Molly's district that most teachers are unsatisfied with the professional development day because it doesn't meet their individual needs or plans. They do not want to participate and often call off work for this day. The day is a contractual workday and a yearly event.

Professional development, when used in education, usually refers to the training that teachers take to improve practice. Much has been written about its ineffectiveness due to the lack of diagnosis (do [all] teachers need this?), delivery, and follow-up (how do we know this was implemented effectively?).

In the past, the committee has arranged a guest speaker and centered the "theme of the day" on the topic to be covered. Usually the speaker pumps up teachers to get excited about teaching. One year, the theme was based on the book *When Fish Fly: Lessons for Creating a Vital and Energized Workplace From the World Famous Pike Place Fish Market* by John Yokoyama and Joseph Michelli (2004). The speaker was a former principal from a high-performing district with a population of students similar to those in Molly's district. He introduced a video clip related to *When Fish Fly* that explained how to turn your workplace into a positive environment in order to find joy in your job. The presentation lasted the entire morning with a 15-minute break in the middle. Molly and her colleagues listened to the speaker and the video, but there was little to no audience participation. The afternoon entailed teacher involvement with different activities based on the grade level they taught, but these activities were not clearly consistent with the book and video. The only follow-up was a survey to ask for opinions about the morning session.

There is no question that presentations and activities like these can be valuable. However, it seemed that there was little practical knowledge to be gained from the experience. Needless to say, this session, just like previous presentations and activities, was not received well by most of Molly's colleagues because it was seen as unnecessary or not helpful in the classroom. In addition, such presentations are usually done in the cafeteria or the school auditorium, neither place being comfortable or conducive to a professional development event.

PROBLEM

Molly's main problem has to do with the fact that one-size-fits-all professional development does little to enhance teacher practice or student learning. Consequently, professional development opportunities are deemed to be a waste of time—many teachers call in sick on these days. Molly is frustrated because her school's teachers look toward her for professional development guidance and support; otherwise they wouldn't have elected her to represent them. The committee reports back to each building asking for input, desires, and needs; however, this input is often ignored because the administrator has his or her own agenda and ultimately overrides the teachers' ideas—this certainly compounds the problem faced by Molly.

PROBING QUESTIONS

1. How can Molly and her committee meet the needs of all the teachers at her school?

2. What needs to be done to improve this professional development experience?

3. Assuming no other money can be raised for professional development, how can the $1,000 best be spent?

MOLLY'S PROPOSED SOLUTION

In most cases, effective school districts offer professional development that represents "focused training" (Marczely, 1996). This kind of training is beneficial when the district wants to implement a wide-scale training of a new approach to teaching or organizational changes within an entire district. It is cost-effective, all teachers gain adequate working knowledge, and implementation is required. Common disadvantages include the fact that it may not be something that meets the needs of teachers as well as that they may oppose the content of training sessions. Many teachers show a particular interest in the instruction-centered training model (Joyce & Showers, 1988) because it directly affects their classroom practice. They also have ample time to reflect on the experience to decide what works for them. Another type of staff development that may be desirable is "self-directed" (Marczely, 1996, pp. 80–87). Teachers identify their goals and put together a plan that allows them to accomplish them. Obviously, teachers are quite likely to be happy with this method of staff development because it meets their needs. However, costs are often a concern, particularly as it is common that school districts choose not to pay for such professional development. It also leaves a lot of responsibility on school administration to monitor that funds are being spent appropriately, and because this model does not limit the choices that teachers have in terms of professional development, it can become an administrative burden to monitor.

It's obvious to Molly and her committee that the type of professional development currently offered by the district is ineffective in the way it is utilized. With this in mind, Molly and her committee develop a plan of action:

- Assuming that the budget for this professional day cannot be changed, the day will be set up as a best-practices event: a day with a series of presentations of what teachers have done in the past year for professional development.
- To prepare for the day, all teachers will write two or three goals for professional development that include short-term and long-term goals at the beginning of the year. They will meet with their administrators to discuss and reflect on their plans, selecting one or two professional workshops, classes, or experiences that will contribute to accomplishing their goals.
- In the meantime, Molly and the professional development committee members will identify teachers within their buildings who will present their professional development activities/experiences. These teachers will be asked to highlight training or experiences that will benefit other teachers within the district. Instead of teachers being forced to sit around listening to a guest speaker on professional development day, they will be asked to attend several presentations or activities that highlight the best professional development experiences. Thus, teachers will be educating teachers, and there will always be a choice of what they want to attend.
- The small $1,000 budget will be used either to provide a breakfast or to choose a venue off school grounds to hold the seminar. By creating and sustaining an inviting professional environment, teachers will feel more like belonging to a professional community.

EXPECTED OUTCOMES

One purpose of staff professional development is to update the skills that staff members have (Hoy & Miskel, 2008). By implementing the proposed type of staff development, districts are able to provide more opportunities for growth without the huge costs associated with other professional development options. Teachers are able to be introduced to a variety of opportunities and can choose which presentations to attend. In addition, the district meets teachers' needs by providing a variety of options, and teachers' peers are the presenters.

A positive response to the program should be expected because there is choice involved and teachers become validated by their peers. By asking teachers to set goals and choose a workshop or class to meet these goals, the school and school district are fostering a good professional growth experience for them. It is always important to give professionals control of their career path, as it increases satisfaction with their careers (Sergiovanni, 2007).

Teachers would also acquire knowledge and develop skills related to best practices that could be used in their classrooms to improve instruction and management. By allowing teachers to share experiences, the district would have a good idea as to what workshops or classes were effective. This would hopefully decrease the money spent on ineffective workshops in the future.

POINTS TO PONDER . . .

How can Molly and her committee's "teacher point of view" help resolve this problem? What other limitations to the current structure and delivery of the annual professional development day are you able to identify? What else could you add to Molly's plan, or how could you improve upon it? How would you be able to involve school administrators in "collective goal setting and decision making"?

QUESTIONS FOR ADMINISTRATORS

Who would be responsible for what in the whole process of implementing the newly created curriculum? How would you promote a participative culture in Molly's district while reinforcing accountability? In addition to the follow-up survey currently in use, what other documentation considerations would you make to evaluate the new curriculum both formatively and summatively? What tools and strategies could you use to validate the new curriculum?

IN-CLASS ACTIVITY

Given your knowledge of Molly's plan, work with two to three others in your class to develop a plan of action that would achieve the following: (a) determine the new curriculum's necessary time allotment and (b) ensure flexible content as well as needs-based scope and sequence.

REFERENCES

Hoy, W. K., & Miskel, C. G. (2008). *Educational administration: Theory, research, and practice* (8th ed.). Boston: McGraw-Hill.

Joyce, B., & Showers, B. (1988). *Student achievement through staff development.* New York: Longman.

Marczely, B. (1996). *Personalizing professional growth: Staff development that works.* Thousand Oaks, CA: Corwin.

Sergiovanni, T. J. (2007). *Rethinking leadership* (2nd ed.). Thousand Oaks, CA: Corwin.

Yokoyama, J., & Michelli, J. (2004). *When fish fly: Lessons for creating a vital and energized workplace from the world famous Pike Place Fish Market.* New York: Hyperion.

SUGGESTED READINGS

Adey, P. (with Hewit, G., Hewitt, J., & Landau, N.). (2004). *The professional development of teachers: Practice and theory.* Boston: Kluwer Academic Publishers.

Guskey, T. R., & Huberman, M. (Eds.). (1995). *Professional development in education: New paradigms and practices.* New York: Teachers College Press.

CASE 17

Using Curriculum Relevance to Motivate Students

Prereading Focus Points: Students have been asking teachers some variation of "When will I ever use this?" probably since the days of Socrates. In this case study, a math teacher decides to do something about eliminating the need for students to ask such questions in her Algebra II class. By connecting the content to the real world, especially to jobs that use the content, she hopes to motivate students.

Level: High school

Content Area: Mathematics

Setting: Suburban

Spotlight on . . .

    a) Motivation; and
    b) Relevance.

Key Terms: Behavioral objectives; learning objectives; constructivism

BACKGROUND INFORMATION ABOUT THE TEACHER

Katy is a high school math teacher in a large suburban school district that has a high graduation rate, and many students go on to 4-year colleges. She teaches three different math courses over five class periods; her five classes are composed of 25 to 32 students each, and two of these classes are Algebra II with college-bound juniors and seniors. These classes are her most challenging because most of these students dislike math and see no reason to learn the more complicated concepts in Algebra II. Katy has been teaching for 6 years, and she is concerned about her students' attitude toward math.

BACKGROUND INFORMATION ABOUT THE CURRICULUM

The current curriculum is based on the nature of the subject matter. Katy's school district is concerned with meeting the goals of state content standards and improving student achievement on state standardized tests. The math curriculum at the high school follows a linear structure where the information builds on itself. Lesson plan structures are product oriented in that objectives and outcomes must match. Objectives within the lesson plans must contain performance goals, conditions, and criteria. The school district favors a behaviorist approach aimed at specific, measurable objectives.

> **Behavioral objectives** are written into lesson plans and describe what the students will do. **Learning objectives** describe what the students will actually learn.

Despite the fact that the curriculum is subject driven, Katy does have some room to work within it. She is given both an outline and a timeline of the specific math concepts at the onset of the school year. A teacher's edition textbook with supplemental materials is provided for her. Katy utilizes cooperative learning, group work, lectures, explorations using technology, and drill/practice teaching methods. Her assessment methods include tests, quizzes, warm-up problems, homework, portfolios, oral reports, and group work activities. She is able to control how the material is presented and the types of assessment given throughout the year; however, Katy must cover a certain amount of material. Her students are given a midterm and final exam that are the same for all the classes in the school. The curriculum for her classes is content driven and based on these exams.

PROBLEM

Matt, an average-achieving Algebra II student, asked the age-old question, "When will I ever need this?" Katy replied, "This is a math concept that you will use in college courses or if you choose to pursue a career in math or science." Matt responded, "I am going to be a communications major. Why do I have to learn it?"

Each day, Katy struggles with how to motivate her students. She feels that students see no connection between what they learn in the classroom and their future lives and the world around them. Since most of her students will attend college, they are willing to accept that they will need math in higher education. Katy wants to find a way to motivate her students to learn about math, as well as to see the connectivity to their lives and, if possible, inspire some of them to enter a mathematics career.

At least once a day, Katy is asked, by students like Matt, the question "When will I ever need this?" She sees Algebra II as a stepping-stone between simple algebra and calculus. Even she believes that there is little functionality, at present, for her students. If her students attend college, they will at least have to retake the Algebra II class. It appears that these students believe that after college they can forget about math and algebra. If they choose a career that requires no math, Katy still would like them to see that members of their community such as coworkers, friends, and other professionals use math and logical thinking. Therefore, she plans to give her students concrete examples of math concepts applied to different careers and hobbies.

PROBING QUESTION

1. How could Katy change the way her math curriculum is implemented to allow the content to become more relevant to her students' lives and more useful in their eyes?

PROPOSED SOLUTION

Katy has several options for implementing changes and adding more relevance into the current curriculum. She can start by presenting to students different careers that use the math concepts included in a given chapter in the textbook. Then she can move on to guiding the students to research for themselves the kinds of jobs that use a specific math idea. Finally, her students should be able to ask a person in a specific profession the right questions to figure out how the math is used in that job. She needs to incorporate the process into her daily lesson plans and assessment.

When a topic is first presented, Katy can describe to her students what jobs use that particular mathematical skill. She can also conduct research online to find specific persons in those careers who utilize a certain concept. At first, she needs to model to her students how she found this information, whether by interviewing, survey, or online research. Then she could present her findings to the whole class in a variety of ways—posters or bulletin boards with pictures or descriptions of the people and how math affects

> **Constructivism** is a way of thinking about how learning takes place. Advocates of this view believe that all of what one learns is done so through the lens of his or her experiences. In other words, none of us is an "empty vessel" into which a teacher can pour knowledge. We must understand all content by negotiating it with what we already know.

their jobs, an oral presentation about the jobs throughout the lesson, or an application problem that would have to be solved by using a particular set of skills in a given profession. After demonstrating how to find the information, Katy could develop a guide to help her students practice finding occupations employing a specific math topic.

Katy should encourage the students to explore the Internet to find occupations that use a math concept. She could take her classes to the computer lab one day or write out directions to help students search online for homework. After the students find jobs that require knowledge of a certain topic, Katy would help the class design a survey. Peer editing and review could be used to refine the interview questions. Students could ask family members, friends, or even community leaders who are in the related professions to answer the questions.

This activity could be incorporated into Katy's assessment plan as a project or an oral presentation. Students' work could be displayed on bulletin boards. Additionally, reflective paragraphs could be included in the portfolio as a way to prompt students to elaborate on their findings about the impact of what they learned on a future career.

The changes that Katy must make to her curriculum will redefine the focus of the material. Although she must still meet the state content standards requirements, she will attempt to shift students' attention to experience instead of content. Dewey's (1938/1997) pragmatism is the belief that curriculum should be centered on a student's experience, reflection, community, interest, and environment. Students will experience through their research projects and reflect using their portfolio artifacts, thus getting involved in the lives of community members and becoming more aware of their own environment. In essence, Katy will take the planned/designed curriculum and change its focus from behaviorism to constructivism. In doing so, she will attempt to make the material meaningful to her students by creating a world that is steeped in mathematics.

EXPECTED OUTCOMES

Katy's goal is to motivate students to learn math, as they need to see that math is relevant to their lives. Her new approach to the curriculum provides her students with the opportunity to construct applications to their lives. She knows that not every student will continue his or her math study past her class or be inspired to pursue a math career. However, she is hoping that by having students participate in these activities, they will learn to appreciate the math in their lives. She will eventually be able to offer relevant examples to support her answer to the seemingly everyday question "When will I ever need this?"

POINTS TO PONDER...

If you were to deal with the same problem as Katy, when do you think your students might be able to attempt answering their own questions about the relevance of curriculum, irrespective of the content area? What would it take for them to be able to be involved in any teacher–student collaborative efforts aimed at increasing the relevance of a given subject matter?

QUESTIONS FOR ADMINISTRATORS

You're a high school assistant principal, and you're in your office after school. Suddenly, the phone rings, and you have a call from a parent who is upset that her child has to take a certain class where the material is seemingly only helpful to advance on to the next level of that content (within the school or into college). How would you respond? Would your response be any different if you were the superintendent of schools?

IN-CLASS ACTIVITY

In content-area groups, brainstorm ideas about a career and how a particular concept from your discipline is used on the job. Develop a visual aid distinguishing among various factors related to the given job: required preparation, a "fun or cool factor" about the job, people students know who might be associated with the job, and so forth.

REFERENCE

Dewey, J. (1997). *Education and experience.* New York: Macmillan. (Original work published 1938)

SUGGESTED READINGS

Daggett, W. (2005). *Achieving academic excellence through rigor and relevance.* Retrieved December 22, 2008, from http://www.leadered.com/pdf/Academic_Excellence.pdf

McNulty, R. J., & Quaglia, R. J. (2007, September). Rigor, relevance, and relationships: Three passwords that unlock the door for engaged high school students to learn at appropriate levels. *The School Administrator*. Retrieved December 22, 2008, from http://www.aasa.org/publications/saarticledetail.cfm?ItemNumber=9330

Authors' Note: "Rigor, Relevance, and Relationships," first coined by the Bill & Melinda Gates Foundation, has been a mantra for high school reform over the past few years. It's hypothesized that we cannot have rigorous coursework without building meaningful relationships with our students and making the content relevant to the learner's life.

CASE 18

The Integration of Autistic Classes Into the Physical Education Curriculum

Prereading Focus Points: A physical education teacher is confronted with meeting the unique yet varied needs of special education students. Not only must she restructure the planned/designed curriculum for her content area, but she also should work against several contextual/structural concerns including the bell schedule and the spaces in the building.

Level: K–8 (elementary and middle school combined)

Content Area: Physical education

Setting: Urban

Spotlight on . . .

    a) Special education; and
    b) Mainstreaming.

Key Terms: Knowledge-centered classrooms; society-centered curricula; mainstreaming

BACKGROUND INFORMATION ABOUT THE TEACHER

Lindsay teaches physical education (PE) in a K–8 elementary school of about 350 students in a large, urban Midwestern school district. Most of the time students receive PE instruction for 50 minutes per week. The school also contains a large special education population, which includes five autistic units comprising an average of 8 students per class. The autistic classrooms are broken down by grade level and not by the physical or mental abilities of the students. Thus the students are often at different points developmentally. These classes are assisted by paraprofessionals who come with the students to PE class.

BACKGROUND INFORMATION ON THE CURRICULUM

In PE, there is a district-prescribed curriculum focusing mainly on the attainment of sports knowledge and skills, which makes for a knowledge-centered classroom. However, because the skills learned in PE are often used outside of class, it may also be viewed as a society-centered curriculum (Ellis, 2004).

PROBLEM

The problem is related to the integration of autistic classes into the physical education curriculum. The scope and sequence given by the district does not often match the development of locomotor skills, nonlocomotor skills, or manipulative skills that the autistic students possess. An example is that Joel, in fourth grade, cannot learn basic basketball skills, as required by the scope and sequence, because he has not yet developed the manipulative skill of throwing a ball. Since the autistic students are grouped by grade level and not developmental ability, there is a wide spectrum of physical abilities within a classroom. Some of the autistic students may be capable of playing modified games at grade-level sequence while others are not able to demonstrate proper running or skipping patterns. It is difficult to follow the district scope and sequence when there is such disparity among the participants in the class. It is also difficult when the skills and abilities that should be taught do not match the motor abilities the students possess.

A second issue for the autistic classrooms is time and space. Since most classes come to PE once a week, it is difficult to establish remembered routines that help autistic students reach a comfort level in a new environment. Thus transitions to gym class are difficult for the autistic students. Another problem for the students is the large space that they are suddenly exposed to. Very often the multipurpose room is in use as they enter or exit. The large space and noise cause distractions and negative behaviors from the autistic students.

A final issue that faces the autistic classes in physical education is the social nature of the curriculum.

> **Knowledge-centered classrooms** are also known as content or teacher centered in contrast to learner centered where the focus of the activities in the classroom is on the student, rather than the teacher. **Society-centered curricula** intend to prepare citizens to meet the needs of the society as a whole. For instance, if more engineers are needed for the economy, science and mathematics will be emphasized.

> Lindsay is involved in **mainstreaming** in that she is teaching students with exceptionalities alongside regular education students. This is an effort to make the classroom more authentic, more real-life to the benefit of all students.

PE by nature causes students to interact with others. Since autism is typified by individual behaviors, it is often difficult for autistic students to participate with others within the context of classes. Autistic students may not be comfortable working with a partner or functioning on a team.

PROBING QUESTIONS

1. What curricular adaptations can be made so that the autistic students understand basic sport concepts but are also able to develop needed locomotor, nonlocomotor, and manipulative skills?

2. What resources can the PE teacher draw upon for ideas and examples in teaching the autistic students?

3. What structures and routines can be in place so that the students are transitioned better into PE?

4. How can autistic students be made more comfortable interacting with others in PE?

PROPOSED SOLUTION

SCOPE AND SEQUENCE ADAPTATION

By adapting the scope and sequence to meet the needs of the learners, the latter can gain basic knowledge of various sports but also work on needed motor skills. One way to accomplish this would be by breaking down the scope and sequence into the basic movement forms such as throwing for basketball and baseball and striking for soccer and hockey. By teaching specific movement forms like striking and throwing, teachers would help the autistic students gain a variety of motor skills that they can use in multiple games. Repetition would also be very important for the autistic students. By focusing not on a particular sport but rather on a movement concept and repeating it, the student would gain the skill and be able to use it in a variety of situations. Through the development of basic motor skills, the autistic students would gain knowledge to use in game situations in the future.

Another way to adapt the curriculum would be to test the students on motor abilities and develop a baseline for the students. Then by grouping students with specific motor abilities, the PE teacher could work on movements where the students are deficient. Students with well-developed movement forms could be challenged by integrating them into game situations. For students who have very developed motor abilities, it may be possible to include them in a regular PE classroom so that they can continue to develop their motor abilities on the appropriate level.

By using resources such as an occupational therapist (OT) or a physical therapist (PT), the PE teacher could also find out other movements that the students have difficulty with and work on developing these movements in class. Very often the OT or PT feels that he or she has inadequate time with the students. By working together, the PE teacher and the therapist may be able to see improvement in the students' motor abilities and movement skills.

TIME AND SPACE

One important aspect for autistic students is the establishment of routines that would begin immediately upon entrance to the room. Routines such as sitting on colored construction paper or putting their jackets in the same place each time would decrease the amount of distractions that autistic students might meet as they enter the new environment. Doing the same warm-ups in the same order might also help transition the students into the new environment. Though the time factor may not be able to be dealt with at the moment, by making every minute count in class the PE teacher can make the most of the little time available. Discussing with the principal the time allotment for PE classes in next year's schedule may influence the time factor in the future.

SOCIAL INTERACTIONS

Since one of the goals of most autistic education is for the students to learn social interactions, the PE classroom is a great place to begin. Introducing low-level games involving social interactions such as tag or throwing a ball to another person would help autistic students become more aware of people around them. By having coordinated group activities as well as free play during a typical class period, students would be challenged to interact with others but also feel individualistic in free play. The teacher may want to challenge certain students to positively interact with the group, while allowing other students to work on their own.

EXPECTED OUTCOMES

By following the plan described above, Lindsay expects her problems to be resolved, as evidenced by the following:

- Students will gain increased locomotor, nonlocomotor, and manipulative skill development, especially for autistic children as noted earlier.
- Improvement in basic skill levels should been seen for all students. Although the plan was designed with the autistic children in mind, all should benefit. Enrichment will come to students whose skills are proficient—those who have basic skill levels should only improve from participating in Lindsay's plan of action.
- All students will develop an awareness of sport knowledge by using the scope and sequence.
- Interaction between the OT or PT and the PE teacher will increase, allowing each to think of his or her work in an interdisciplinary manner, as well as to think about how to improve collegiality and promote collaborative curricular and instructional problem solving.
- Lindsay also expects a decrease in disruptions that were due to transitioning into PE class.
- One of the most important aspects of teaching is relationships between students and teachers—building and maintaining trust. This plan will allow Lindsay more opportunities for social interactions with students.

POINTS TO PONDER . . .

Based on Lindsay's careful planning, do you see any other benefits to students (autistic and nonautistic), teachers, parents, or the school in general that might be received if the proposed measures are implemented? How might you argue that Lindsay's plan is society centered in that it benefits society as a whole?

QUESTIONS FOR ADMINISTRATORS

As a principal of Lindsay's K–8 school, how would you support her in this endeavor? How would you communicate this support and the plan to parents and the community? What do you think would be necessary to inform the school district about the outcomes of these actions, possibly leading to districtwide adoption or adaptation?

IN-CLASS ACTIVITY

In groups of two or three in similar content areas and/or grade levels, brainstorm ideas for mainstreaming students with learning exceptionalities.

Consider how you would deliver content, group students, manage behavior, and assess what students have learned. Also, highlight some of the potential problems you would be likely to encounter in the process.

REFERENCE

Ellis, A. K. (2004). *Exemplars of curriculum theory.* Larchmont, NY: Eye on Education.

SUGGESTED READING

Davis, K. (1990). *Adapted physical education for students with autism.* Springfield, IL: Charles C Thomas Publishers.

Author's Note: Also see the National Association for Sport & Physical Education Web site (http://www.aahperd.org/naspe/), which has up-to-date information pertaining to children who are physically challenged.

Developing a Literacy Program for Children With Learning Disabilities

Prereading Focus Points: Teaching literacy to a large (by exceptional student education standards) class of students with many learning disabilities proves to be a challenge. The teacher takes it upon herself to develop a literacy program based on the learning styles of her students.

Level: Elementary school

Content Area: Special education

Setting: Suburban

Spotlight on . . .
   a) Learning styles; and
   b) Program development.

Key Terms: Socioeconomic status (SES); leveled books; learning style

BACKGROUND INFORMATION ABOUT THE TEACHER

Mae has been a licensed special education teacher of fourth- through sixth-grade students with learning disabilities since she left her teacher education program at a large public university 4 years ago. Mae works with a group of students who participate in individual small-group instruction daily. This instruction is provided at a suburban public intermediate school that has a mid-to-high range of socioeconomic levels including students who receive free lunch. Mae's class is unevenly distributed by gender (boys 10, girls 7), and all 17 students are together

> **Socioeconomic status (SES) is** determined by a student's parent or guardian's level of education and income. The percentage of students receiving free or reduced lunch is the most common way of measuring SES in schools.

in the resource room for language arts instruction. Thirteen of the students are fourth graders while the other 4 students are fifth graders. These 17 students with learning disabilities have different learning preferences that impact their success in schools.

BACKGROUND INFORMATION ABOUT THE CURRICULUM

Mae's curriculum is derived from the regular education curriculum as well as her state's academic content standards for grades 4–6. The standards provide a set of clear and rigorous expectations for all students and provide teachers with clearly defined statements of what students should know and be able to do as they progress through school. Mae does modify how the curriculum is taught in order for the students to be successful. Some of the modifications she uses are **leveled books** (books designated to be written for specific reading levels), tests read orally to students, small-group instruction, graphic organizers, and books on tape. Her lesson plans are well structured; they begin with learning objectives, a well-chosen activity, and an evaluation to see how her students are doing. Mae believes in having attainable, real-world goals so that what's learned in class can be used by her students in their lives.

PROBLEM

Mae is getting frustrated planning for her language arts class because she has 17 students with learning disabilities and many different styles of learning. Her lessons have become very complex because she has to meet a variety of needs in only an hour's time. Mae is trying to accommodate for the students using lessons that seemed to work in the past with other students. She feels that students are not experiencing success in their learning. Mae knows something has to change. Therefore, she asks herself, "How do educators develop a literacy program for children with learning disabilities?" It is hard enough for regular education teachers to try and create literacy programs that will maintain and develop the interests of regular education students. To develop a program for children with learning disabilities and children with severe disabilities seems impossible. Mae wonders if she could use students' learning styles as a planning tool for literacy instruction for students with learning disabilities, as children with learning disabilities have a harder time learning to read and write than do regular education children.

> **Learning style** refers to the preferred or most effective way in which a person learns. This can be in the form of auditory, kinesthetic, or visual.

1. Is a literacy program that incorporates all learning styles a more effective way to teach children with disabilities?

PROPOSED SOLUTION

Different literacy programs are readily available that can be used for children with learning disabilities. The way in which a student takes in new information and sorts, retains, retrieves, and reproduces it depends heavily on the student's style of learning. Students take in and process information by seeing and hearing, reflecting and acting, and analyzing and visualizing. Three main styles of learning are auditory, kinesthetic, and visual (Gardner, 1993). Auditory learners learn best by hearing the material. Kinesthetic learners prefer doing, and visual learners need to see the material to learn most effectively. Most students use a combination of all three modalities. Teachers should be aware of students' learning styles and develop a literacy program that is balanced and meets the needs of all students in the classroom. For example, teachers can use such things as audiotapes and lectures for auditory learners. Kinesthetic learners would benefit from taking notes, rewriting, technology (which also helps visual learners), and hands-on activities. Visual learners would benefit from teachers using text, film strips, pictures, charts, and graphs. To further Mae's literacy program she would need to make sure that she emphasizes writing and reading activities that are directed toward students with learning disabilities.

Such students often have a deficit in one or more of these modalities and as a result prefer one modality over another. Using a teaching approach that includes the three learning styles will assist all students, regular and special education, in learning the class material more effectively. A literacy program that uses a combination of teaching styles (based on students' learning styles) will enhance learning within the classroom. The role of the teacher is to work with students to incorporate all styles of learning into the literacy program to improve performance of all students and address the needs of all students. This can be achieved by developing a comprehensive knowledge of students' learning styles by means of an informal survey. If students indicate they are visual learners, teachers should include pictures, film strips, charts, and graphs to enhance learning. Teachers should not teach exclusively in their students' preferred modalities. Students may not develop "mental dexterity" (skills in other modalities they need to reach their potential for achievement in school and as professionals).

An objective for teachers is to help students build skills in their preferred as well as their less preferred styles of learning. Using a program like this seems to incorporate the different learning styles essential for all learners. These programs would work well in an inclusive setting where all the children can have the opportunity to participate. Reading instruction for children with special needs must be able to change in occurrence to the styles of learning that these students have. Mae should keep the beginnings simple and progress as her students' awareness progresses. The last two—and the most important—factors of this program are (a) growing avenues of communication and (b) taking time for learning.

EXPECTED OUTCOMES

Children with learning disabilities whose teachers address different learning styles should exhibit significantly higher achievement than those students whose teachers do not. A literacy program that uses all styles of learning could be applied to all students in a variety of subject areas. While further research is needed in other subject areas, the suggested benefits to students' learning achievement warrant teachers to try this instructional method in their classrooms. In teaching instruction today it is very important that teachers take advantage of all tools available to increase student motivation and achievement.

POINTS TO PONDER . . .

Mae is a very motivated, caring teacher. Not every teacher, unfortunately, may have the time and other resources to develop a program such as the one described in the proposed solution. What resources might you tap into if you were in a similar situation? How would you propose managing the time and other resources necessary to develop such a program?

QUESTIONS FOR ADMINISTRATORS

How would you support the work of Mae if you were her principal? What resources might you make available to her? Assume you don't have readily available funds to purchase an expensive software program. How might you secure such funds?

IN-CLASS ACTIVITY

In a small group based on the same content area or grade level, develop a 45-minute set of instruction that would address the three modalities that are mentioned in Mae's case study (visual, auditory, and kinesthetic).

REFERENCE

Gardner, H. (1993). *Frames of mind: The theory of multiple intelligences.* New York: Basic Books.

SUGGESTED READING

National Institute for Literacy. (n.d.). *Literacy & learning disabilities special collection* (LINCSearch). Retrieved December, 23, 2008, from http://ldlink.coe.utk.edu/home.htm

My Students Can't Write, and I'm Forced to Use a Curriculum That Doesn't Help Them Learn How

Prereading Focus Points: A kindergarten teacher in an urban setting was thrown into the profession without sufficient preparation due to a teaching shortage. She intuitively found solutions to the problems she confronted, especially that her students were at varying, but usually low, levels of writing ability in her kindergarten classroom. She decided to stray from the mandated, scripted curriculum and find alternatives that she deemed a better fit for her students and her academically and racially diverse classroom. It wasn't until years later that she was able to make the connections between what she had implemented and sound curriculum theory.

Level: Elementary school

Content Area: English-language arts

Setting: Urban

Spotlight on . . .

    a) Mandated curriculum; and
    b) Diverse needs of students.

Key Terms: Emergency teaching credentialing; teacher-centered; learner-centered; *Open Court Reading*

BACKGROUND INFORMATION ABOUT THE TEACHER

Patricia has been a kindergarten teacher at an urban elementary school in a large West Coast school district for over 10 years. She started off her career as a day-to-day substitute teacher and then decided she wanted to work full-time. Patricia

Emergency teaching credentialing often occurs in urban settings where it's difficult to find licensed teachers to battle the challenges of inner-city schooling. A typical way to credential is to bring in someone who ostensibly has the content knowledge, give her a class or classes of children, and expect her to "figure out" teaching as she goes along. Often this involves taking courses at night and/or assigning a helpful (or not-so-helpful) veteran teacher to act as mentor.

was able to teach on an emergency credential while going to school in the evening—due to a teacher shortage in the area. The school she works at is predominantly African American, and when she first started teaching there, Patricia believed this to be a wonderful opportunity for her to expand her knowledge about the culture. She considered herself a progressive person but traditional when it came to how she thought about teaching. Not only did Patricia learn a lot while going to graduate school and getting her teaching credential, but she also had a wonderful language arts coach, as mentoring was provided to all new teachers by the district. The coach reminded her to learn that she did not just teach from the teacher's guide, so together they explored different styles of teaching. This mentoring was critical in helping Patricia develop the daily journal writing program that she implemented her first year of teaching kindergarten upon which she continued to improve each year.

The language arts program Patricia and the aide assigned to her classroom used during the time of this case study was very controversial because many teachers felt it was too scripted. But due to the transient nature of the student population in the district, this program was a good choice for Patricia's particular situation. If a child happened to move schools three times in a school year, she could at least be sure her language arts curriculum would be consistent. Patricia knew it was not for everyone, but she tried to find ways to be creative, and using the program actually taught her quite a bit about teaching language arts. As Patricia became familiar with curriculum scholars in her graduate course several years later, she found that many different types of curriculum were actually incorporated into this daily journal writing program.

A central strategy was the use of learning centers, which Patricia implemented for an hour each day when she divided the children into three groups of six or seven for 20-minute rotations. (Her district does not permit more than 20 students per classroom teacher for grades K–3. If the school exceeds this limit, it will be fined by the state, and its funding will be reduced.) One group did journal writing with the teacher while the other two groups did either math, science, or a follow-up to the language arts whole-group lesson. Patricia's aide and a colleague with whom she was team teaching facilitated each of these groups. When she could get parent volunteers, Patricia would have them assist with one of these groups.

BACKGROUND INFORMATION ABOUT THE CURRICULUM

The kind of curriculum approach that Patricia took is a combination of a few different models. The prescribed curriculum required both **teacher-centered** and **learner-centered** instruction. Regarding the latter: "This means an environment in which opportunities for self-realization are abundant . . . meeting the needs and interest of the individual learner by giving the learner opportunities to explore, to follow his/her curiosities, and to exercise personal choice and responsibility" (Ellis, 2004, p. 41). But Patricia also was to use a more traditional, teacher-centered way to teach based on *Open Court* as her language arts program. "*Open Court Reading* is a research-based curriculum grounded in systematic, explicit instruction of phonemic awareness, phonics and word knowledge, comprehension skills and strategies, inquiry skills and strategies, and writing and language arts skills and strategies" (U.S. Department of Education Institute of Education Sciences [IES], 2008). The program in question also features journal writing as part of the curriculum.

PROBLEM

Every Friday, Patricia did something called "Seminar." Regarding this strategy, Ellis (2004, p. 135) states, "The teacher leads the seminar but must do so by playing the role of questioner, thought provoker, and drawer-out. . . . Students must participate actively, using arguments drawn from knowledge they have acquired and critically examined." Patricia found this quite easy to do with kindergarten-aged children. The teacher must lead the seminar and model for the children how they are to conduct this activity, so she would sit in a big circle and ask them to share one of their journal entries for the week. A volunteer would then show his or her work and "read" what had been written. Two students would next respond to the first child's writing, either by making a positive statement about the journal entry, such as "I really like the way you drew your house," or by asking a question, such as "What is your sister's name?" Patricia would not only model for the students but also redirect or refocus them whenever necessary.

This activity served many functions. It provided a format for the children to showcase their work as well as see what their peers were doing. It helped not only with the written word but also with the spoken, as students had to learn how to articulate what they were saying. It was a long, tedious process in the beginning, but the end result was well worth waiting for.

The reason such a rigorous writing program was implemented at such a young age is because *children were entering first grade unable to write*, Patricia emphasized. They were only able to write their names and print the alphabet. They could often copy information off of the board, but teachers wanted them to be able to communicate their own thoughts and put their own ideas onto paper. Patricia and the other kindergarten teachers at her school agreed that it is never too early to learn, so they started a daily journal writing program that gave the children an opportunity to explore their own thoughts and ideas while learning the "rules" of the written language. They firmly believed that children meet teachers' expectations.

However, whenever she introduced this program to parents at "Back-to-School Night," where teachers would review their curriculum for the year, Patricia was often met with chuckles. Even at her first parent conferences several weeks later, the parents often did not understand the purpose of some of her strategies (inventive spelling, for instance, described below) and were wondering when she was actually going to teach them how to learn as they had done in school.

PROBING QUESTIONS

1. How should teachers model proper writing for young learners through the use of journaling?

2. How should teachers encourage students to begin the writing process?

3. How should teachers encourage children to think of their own writing topics?

ACTUAL SOLUTION

Even though the prescribed curriculum seemed to have a balance of teacher- and learner-centered aspects, Patricia and her colleagues felt that they needed to accentuate the learner-centered in order to meet with success. Using this model was not just about what children would be able to produce by rote memorization but rather was about teachers fostering critical thinking and helping students develop ways of learning. Specific to her own classroom, Patricia proposed to *implement a daily journal writing program where children are encouraged to explore their own thoughts and ideas.* Positive reinforcement of the individual's level of writing is required in order to keep the child engaged and striving to achieve more. Inventive spelling is a must at this age as most children are unable to even write each letter of the alphabet, much less know each sound and the rules of spelling.

Patricia would model her performance expectations once students got to their journal writing table. Their first journal was written onto white art paper with no lines. Patricia would "write" her first journal entry onto a large piece of paper for the children to see. She wanted to convey excitement as she kicked off this writing process with the class. They really liked seeing their name on the journal. Patricia often modeled something for them that they could relate to, like a picture of her own bedroom. They were not required to also draw a picture of their bedroom, but at that young age it is important to give them some place to begin, according to Patricia. Later they would have more confidence to create their own writing topics. She often encouraged them to write about something the class was learning or reading about. Using the bedroom example, she would sound out "bedroom" with the class and, depending on their responses or level of spelling, would write out either the word or just "BDRM." Children at this age have various levels of writing skills. While one child may be able to spell the entire word, others may not be able to even write a single letter. Patricia usually emphasized just writing the sounds they heard.

The children would continue to write in the plain-paged journal for several weeks. Patricia would then have them "read" their journal entry to her, and she would write what they said or write a comment about their journal including the words they had used to "read" it to her. It seemed of great interest to them when they could see the words they had spoken. The level of their writing skills would help determine what the teacher wrote. Patricia tried writing comments or questions that would elicit a one- or two-word response, such as:

- I love your bedroom!
- Do you share a room with your sister or brother?
- Who else sleeps in your bedroom with you?
- What color are the walls in your bedroom?

As time went on, the children expected and anticipated the interactive writing in their journals. Some students, depending on how much time was left, were able to answer the question Patricia had asked. Others would merely copy her sentence. Patricia would usually accept any form of writing at this level. It was also acceptable if the student saw a word in the sentence she had written and then rewrote that word. Patricia tried to make her sentences or questions very simple so that it was easy for them to follow what she was writing.

The next journal Patricia gave them would have a large space on the top for drawing a picture and then some lines for them to write on. She also made a big deal out of their getting journals with lines and would model for several days what she expected. Patricia asked that they draw a picture first and then write about the picture. Sometimes she needed to use a timer to limit the amount of time the children spent drawing. At this stage Patricia usually got a lot of "I can't write" responses, prompting her to go back and show them that they actually could write. They may not have been at the same level as their peers, but *they could write!* It was a long, time-consuming process, but the end result was rewarding. Parents did not necessarily agree with her method because they thought she was encouraging poor spelling skills, but she tried to assure them that their children would have plenty of time to learn how to spell.

Once the students became more familiar with their journaling process and their confidence increased, Patricia would start to introduce punctuation and capitalization. With such an informal way to teach, she found she could cater her comments to each child. If she saw that a child was starting to write in complete sentences, Patricia would talk to her about capitalizing the first letter of the sentence. Journal writing was also found to be a nice time to review letter sound skills with the children.

Patricia would then group the children into sets of about six, not by any particular academic level. Grouping them into smaller groups was more manageable because she could take the time to work with each child. Parent volunteers facilitated learning centers, as Patricia focused on journal writing instruction.

Patricia would never allow erasers in kindergarten and especially at the journal table. Children of this age are quite occupied with making mistakes, and she would always tell them that in their journals there are no mistakes as long as they continue to try.

OBSERVED OUTCOMES

As a result of implementing the proposed curricular change, the kindergarten children were better prepared to begin their first-grade year not only as exploratory writers but as critical thinkers. They were able to complete a task on their own from start to finish with some guidelines but with the ability to creatively think of a topic and to write about it on their own. This curricular change allowed the children to critically think as opposed to simply regurgitate information that was given to them. Academic rigor was always important to Patricia and her colleagues, and that meant expecting high-quality work from their students. Journal writing fostered visual art, speech, storytelling, and reading skills in their young children. Parents soon saw how enjoyable this was for their children and the real results that this journal writing program brought.

POINTS TO PONDER . . .

What would you have done differently if in Patricia's situation? How would you align such a journal writing project with state content standards? Are there any ways in which you could promote writing across curriculum for such young learners?

QUESTIONS FOR ADMINISTRATORS

As principal of Patricia's school, how would you support her given that the district insisted on the mandated curriculum and the parents were initially skeptical of her methods? Assume the role of the district curriculum director— if the principal and teachers at a school in your district claimed that the curriculum you recommended and purchased was not useful, how would you react?

IN-CLASS ACTIVITY

In small groups decide how you would approach your principal if you were given a mandated curriculum that you did not support. How would you argue your position? If you took a stance to not teach this curriculum, how would you explain it to the parents? What evidence would you need, and how might you collect it? Answer these questions in outline form to be presented to your colleagues in class.

REFERENCES

Ellis, A. K. (2004). *Exemplars of curriculum theory*. Larchmont, NY: Eye on Education.
U.S. Department of Education Institute of Education Sciences (IES). (2008, August). *Open court reading*. Retrieved April 15, 2009, from http://ies.ed.gov/ncee/wwc/reports/beginning_reading/open_court/

SUGGESTED READINGS

Duke, N. K. (2003). Reading to learn from the very beginning: Information books in early childhood. *Young Children, 58*(2), 14–20. Retrieved February 24, 2009, from http://www.journal.naeyc.org/btj/200303/InformationBooks.pdf

Roskos, K. A., Christie, J. F., & Richgels, D. J. The essentials of early literacy instruction. *Young Children, 58*(2), 58–60. Retrieved February 24, 2009, from http://www.journal.naeyc.org/btj/200303/Essentials.pdf

Author's Note: Also see *The Journal of Early Childhood Literacy* Web site at http://ecl.sagepub.com/.

Meeting the Needs of Diverse Learners and the Mandates of Accountability Without Compromising

Prereading Focus Points: Teachers often struggle to find a curriculum model with which they agree—one that matches their teaching style and philosophy of how learning takes place. And it's even a bigger struggle to find a school that supports this vision. Once they have found both, you'd think that they would be set, but in this age of accountability, this may not be the case. Mandates from sources located far from where the learning takes place (each individual classroom) can alter what and how a teacher teaches and what and how students learn—or don't learn. This case study offers us a chance to see how such a situation impacts the practice of a thoughtful, motivated mathematics teacher and how she alters her practice to meet these mandates while keeping true to her beliefs. Her efforts are an attempt to ensure that deep understanding takes place in a culturally, racially, linguistically, and economically diverse school.

Level: K–12

Content Area: Mathematics

Setting: Urban

Spotlight on . . .

   a) Accountability;
   b) Teacher empowerment; and
   c) Achievement Gap.

Key Terms: Theme-based schools and curriculum; non-in-depth learning; higher-order learning; Achievement Gap

BACKGROUND INFORMATION ABOUT THE TEACHER

Theme-based schools and curriculum use a broad theme such as fantasy around which all learning takes place. This is done to enhance the connections between content areas (curriculum coherence) and as a way to motivate students to learn.

Valentina was recently hired as a mathematics teacher at a public "fantasy" school with 560 students in an economically distressed, ethnically diverse urban area. Teaching is her third career, and as a member of a cultural minority, she feels she has a lot to offer to her students. The school is considered a "melting pot," as all 560 students are at least bilingual, and they come from different social classes and cultures. Many learners have special needs, while others are identified as gifted and talented. The teachers hold firmly to a commitment that all of their children will have an equal opportunity to learn regardless of background.

Typically, students learn through direct instruction; textbooks; hands-on experience; and easy-to-use, online, school-supported supplemental materials. Tutoring is available around a student's schedule. The math classrooms (same as other subjects) are broken down by the grade level of the students. The school's five content standards for teaching mathematics are the following:

1. Numbers and Operations

2. Algebra

3. Geometry

4. Measurement and Data Analysis

5. Probability

To meet the different needs of students, the school differentiates instruction, basing it on the needs of each of its uniquely diverse students.

BACKGROUND INFORMATION ABOUT THE CURRICULUM

A district-prescribed math curriculum is designed to help students unlock their full academic potential and achieve mastery of the concepts and skills they will need to succeed in life. The curriculum is also intended to provide high-caliber education exceeding the expectations of students, parents, and employers. The curriculum focuses on the achievement of knowledge and skills, sharing them efficiently, helping other students create meaning by engaging in stimulating experiences, and ultimately creating a just society. In Valentina's school, all students receive the opportunity and adequate support to learn mathematics regardless of their personal characteristics, backgrounds, or physical challenges.

The school's math teachers follow a coherent curriculum articulated across grade levels, focused on what they believe to be "important" mathematics that will prepare their students for the world outside of school as well as the next grade level. Valentina and her colleagues believe in building instruction around "mathematical ideas," both in the curriculum and in daily classroom instruction. It is their job to help students see that mathematics is an integrated whole, not a list of isolated fragments and pieces, and that these ideas gain significance when they are useful in the development of other ideas, link ideas one to another, or serve to illustrate the discipline of mathematics as a human challenge.

Effective mathematics teaching in this theme-based school requires understanding of what students know and need to learn and then challenging and supporting them to learn well. What students learn depends more or less on the experiences that mathematics teachers provide every day in the classroom. Valentina's actions are what actually encourage students to think, question, solve problems, and discuss their ideas, strategies, and solutions. She believes it to be her job to suggest that all students learn mathematics with understanding, actively building new knowledge from experience and prior knowledge.

The school's curriculum supports the learning of important mathematical facts and concepts. Feedback from daily assessments helps students set goals for themselves and thus become more independent learners. Additionally, these assessment tools assist Valentina in making pertinent instructional decisions. In this light, she uses a variety of techniques based on which she can interpret accurately how her students may be thinking mathematically. The school district prescribes a large number of tests connected to the curriculum; at the same time, students are also subject to mandatory state exams.

As described in the district curriculum manual, technology is crucial in teaching and learning mathematics. Calculators and computers are essential tools for doing and learning mathematics in the classroom. Technology allows students with special needs to bypass less important procedures so that important mathematics can be considered.

PROBLEM

Evaluation of students is based on a large number of quizzes and tests followed by the state exam, which creates a lot of pressure on everyone involved: superintendents, principals, and teachers. The latter feel enormous pressure to raise test scores at all costs. For teachers with little or no experience who strictly follow the curriculum standards, it is very difficult to adopt the student-centered approach to mathematics and the teaching of mathematics.

Additionally, the mandatory textbook and its corresponding curriculum materials are often not well aligned with state standards. This too often results in excessive drill, review, and practice tests, which make the students very unhappy, crushing motivation to learn.

> **Non-in-depth understanding** versus **higher-order learning**: Valentina and her colleagues would like their students to learn at higher levels as described in Bloom's (1956) *Taxonomy of Cognitive Development*.

Focusing on the state mathematics standards, they contain a large number of mathematical topics to be covered in a short period of time, thus leading to *non-in-depth understanding*. In addition, limited teaching and learning time particularly affects students with different capabilities in understanding the subject.

Typically, Valentina is supposed to spend a small portion of a lesson explaining or reviewing an idea and then go into "production mode." In the production mode students often make their way with difficulty through a set of exercises due to insufficient time. What happens next is that she finds herself going from desk to desk reteaching and explaining the same thing to students. This is a significant contrast to a lesson built around a single problem, the typical approach for student-centered problem-based instruction that the teachers in her school favor. Therefore, the students who struggle the most due to the insufficient teaching and learning time are, in Valentina's estimate, those who are impoverished. And if the time constraints continue to become more severe, the gifted and talented students—a significant portion of Valentina's class—may lose interest.

PROBING QUESTION

1. The teaching time is spread equally for all mathematic subjects. What curriculum adaptations can be made so the students can learn mathematics with deep understanding and higher-order learning?

ACTUAL SOLUTION

Soon after she started her job, it became clear to Valentina that the Achievement Gap does not decrease by simply increasing the number of tests. At a diverse school like hers, there is a need for a shift from a teacher-centered to a child-centered approach in mathematical instruction, a belief that also supports the school's philosophy. She encourages the gifted students to sit next to the students with attention deficit hyperactivity disorder or the ones with low performance to work as a group. To make certain that no student is left behind in learning mathematics, tutoring is provided after a teacher-focused lesson.

To avoid reteaching the students due to the short time allotted, Valentina uses a three-part lecture strategy: "before, during, and after." In the "before" phase, she ensures that the problem at hand is understood, activates useful prior knowledge, and establishes clear expectations for outcomes. In the "during" phase, Valentina avoids stepping into the struggle, listens carefully, and provides appropriate hints while carefully observing and evaluating. In the "after" phase, which is usually a class discussion, she encourages her students to talk about the problem. In doing so, she accepts students' solutions without evaluation, allowing them to summarize the main ideas and identify future problems. Often, these three-part lessons are built around a single problem or task. It is quite easy to dedicate approximately one hour (a full class) to

> The **Achievement Gap** is a commonly used phrase referring to the differences between nonminority and some minority (especially African American and Latino) students in standardized test scores and other measures of school success.

one problem, but there are times when a task may not take a full mathematics lesson. A mental mathematics or oral drill activity is a good example. During these occasions, Valentina improvises shorter, more easily solved problems.

To bring out the best in all of her students during what Valentina calls her lectures (modeling done in front of the whole class), she uses the following strategies:

- Write and orally state the content language objectives.
- Explain the context and use any appropriate visuals to help students understand the task she wants them to solve.
- Simplify the sentence structure and limit the use of nonessential vocabulary, especially technological vocabulary.

OBSERVED OUTCOMES

The following are results Valentina noticed as a result of having implemented the plan described above:

- With the decrease in the numbers of tests, students are more focused and less frustrated.

- Academic performance has increased, and the school seems to be a better place for students.
- With the adjusted lecture time, Valentina is better able to meet the various needs of her students.

According to quiz and test results, basic skill level was reached by all diversified students and enrichment provided to promising students. From her perspective, not only are students now motivated to learn, discuss, and come up with their own solutions to problems, but they have also learned to work together as a group, and a better class community has been created.

POINTS TO PONDER...

Valentina believes she's found solutions to her problem of teaching mathematics in a highly diverse classroom and working through the mandates of frequent testing. How could teachers be successful in similar academically diverse classrooms? How could teachers work through the pressures of high-stakes mandates to do what they feel is best for their students without feeling like they are compromising academic rigor and integrity?

QUESTIONS FOR ADMINISTRATORS

As a principal, would you support Valentina's approach to teaching higher-level thinking skills? What may be some problems you foresee in implementing such a plan across one department or even the whole school? Focusing on state mandates, as a site-based or district administrator, how would you deal with mandates with which you do not quite agree? What might be the consequences of such resistance?

IN-CLASS ACTIVITY

In a content- or grade level–based group, discuss the issue of "teacher empowerment"—what are some of the pros and cons to it? How should teachers approach the process of empowering themselves and their peers? At the same time, how should they deal with differences within a diverse teaching staff when it comes to empowering every one of them? On a T-chart note the problems as well as facilitators that you think teachers like Valentina and her colleagues should be aware of.

REFERENCES

Bloom, B. S. (1956). *Taxonomy of educational objectives: The classification of educational goals.* New York: Susan Fauer Company.

Oakes, J. (1985). *Keeping track: How schools structure inequality.* New Haven, CT: Yale University Press.

University of Connecticut Neag Center for Gifted Education and Talent Development. (n.d.). *The National Research Center on the Gifted and Talented (NRC/GT).* Retrieved June 19, 2009, from http://www.gifted.uconn.edu/NRCGT.html

SUGGESTED READINGS

Donovan, M. S., & Cross, C. T. (Eds.). (2003). *Minority students in special and gifted education.* Washington, DC: National Academy of Sciences, Committee on Minority Representation in Special Education.

Gardner, H. (1998, Winter). A multiplicity of intelligences. *Scientific American Presents: Exploring Intelligence, 9*(4), 18–23.

Glossary

Achievement Gap: A commonly used phrase referring to the differences between nonminority and some minority (especially African American and Latino) students in standardized test scores and other measures of school success.

Action research: A form of research involving a primary investigator (in education it is usually the classroom teacher) and a participant in the study's environment; an effort to link relevant theory and effective practice.

Advanced Placement (AP) courses: College-bound courses that are content-driven curricula for students who demonstrate the required level of cognitive performance to be successful in classrooms using this rigorous system.

Affective learning: Students demonstrate a range of emotional intensity as a reaction to stimuli is considered.

Assessment mapping: The procedure that outlines the connections among assessment tools, student performance, and the instructional activities designed to help students meet set objectives.

Authentic assessment: A way of measuring what students know based on correlations between classroom-based learning and opportunities for application of knowledge to real-life situations.

Balanced curriculum: A system of curriculum with a strong correlation among standards, subject matter content, and assessment based on a structure that allows for monitoring of student progress, teacher input, and curriculum revisions.

Behavioral objectives: What a teacher believes a student will be able to do based on what is to be learned. A key component of many lesson plans (see "learning objectives").

Connoisseurship model (Eisner, 1979): Curriculum theory that relies on empirical evidence leading to appreciation of what is significant in educational settings.

Constructivism: A way of thinking about how learning takes place. Those who are advocates of this view believe that all of what one learns is done so through the lens of his or her experiences. In other words, none of us is an "empty vessel" into which a teacher can pour knowledge. We must understand all content by negotiating it with what we already know.

Continuous Improvement Plan (CIP): A document that connects the mission and vision statements, as well as specific benchmarks and indicators, at the district level with strengths, areas of improvement, actions, expected outcomes, and a timeline at the school level.

Curriculum alignment: A complex process by which content standards correlate with subject matter content, instructional strategies and materials, learning opportunities, assessment tools, and evidence of student learning, thus leading to improved student performance.

Curriculum mapping: A complex process by which curricula are analyzed in terms of how their sequence over the academic calendar correlates with student learning assessment data.

D.A.R.E. (Drug Abuse Resistance Education): A highly acclaimed program offered to schoolchildren from kindergarten to 12th grade, featuring police officers participating actively in classrooms to address coping effectively with issues such as peer pressure, gang activity, violence, and drug/substance abuse.

Discovery learning: A process in which students acquire knowledge about their physical and/or social environment by engaging in firsthand interactions with its various components.

Emergency teaching credentialing: This often occurs in urban settings where it is difficult to find licensed teachers to battle the challenges of inner-city schooling. A typical way to credential is to bring in someone who ostensibly has the content knowledge, give her a class or classes of children, and expect her to "figure out" teaching as she goes along. Often this involves taking courses at night and/or assigning a helpful (or not-so-helpful) veteran teacher to act as mentor.

Enduring understandings: A way of learning that transfers knowledge ("big ideas") beyond the realm of the classroom.

Enrichment Triad: A curriculum model in gifted and talented education that features three interrelated types of enrichment activities focused on general exploration, group training, and individual as well as small-group investigations of real-life problems.

Essential questions: A teaching strategy that leads to the uncovering of the complexity of an academic discipline by means of inquiry on the part of students.

Even Start Family Literacy programs: A system that partners schools and their communities in an attempt to address issues such as poverty and illiteracy by means of aligning early childhood education, adult literacy, and parenting education.

Favored practice: A teaching strategy that we are most comfortable using even if it does or does not improve learning in our classroom.

Hidden curriculum: Essentially, anything that students learn without any evidence of or requirement for it according to the planned or intended school curriculum.

Higher-order learning: As described in Bloom's (1956) Taxonomy of Cognitive Development, the levels of analysis, synthesis, and evaluation constitute higher-level understanding/cognition (see "non-in-depth understanding").

"Highly Qualified Teacher" (HQT): A portion of the No Child Left Behind Act of 2002 that requires schools to ensure that teachers have the necessary content-area and pedagogical knowledge to teach in the context in which they are placed. HQT varies from state to state.

Inner-ring suburb: A city located adjacent to a much larger, highly urbanized city. It often has the same characteristics as the larger city including similar socioeconomic status of its inhabitants. An outer-ring and/or exurb, by contrast, is usually a wealthier, "bedroom" community farther away from the central city.

Invisible culture: The sum of all aspects of one's cultural characteristics not available to conscious awareness.

Knowledge-centered (also known as content- or teacher-centered) **classrooms:** Classrooms in which teaching strategies are used where the focus of the activities is on the content to be learned, rather than the student (see "learner-centered").

Learner-centered: "This means an environment in which opportunities for self-realization are abundant . . . meeting the needs and interest of the individual learner by giving the learner opportunities to explore, to follow his/her curiosities, and to exercise personal choice and responsibility" (Ellis, 2004, p. 41) (see "knowledge-centered classrooms").

Learning objectives: A section of a lesson plan that describes what the student will actually learn, usually described in terms of Bloom's Taxonomy of Cognitive Development (see "behavioral objectives").

Learning style: The preferred or most effective way in which a person learns. This can be in the form of auditory, kinesthetic, or visual.

Leveled books: Books designated to be written for specific reading levels.

Levy: A change in millage usually requiring a public vote campaign (see "mill").

"Looping" (also known as "continuity of caring"): Following a group of students for 2 or more years instead of the students having a different teacher or set of teachers each academic year.

Mainstreaming: The placement of students with exceptionalities alongside regular education students. This is an effort to make the classroom more authentic, more real-life to the benefit of all students.

Mill: This is one one-thousandth of a dollar and is used in reference to the property tax rate percentage that is to be assessed for individual homeowners. Typically one half of a school district's income is derived from property taxes, and a levy is needed to be accepted by voters in order to increase the mills assessed (see "levy").

Multiple intelligences: The core of a theory generated by Howard Gardner (1983) who claimed that IQ scores alone cannot reveal an individual's true set of abilities. Gardner has identified eight intelligences: bodily-kinesthetic, interpersonal, intrapersonal, verbal-linguistic, logical-mathematical, naturalistic, visual-spatial, and musical.

Non-in-depth understanding: As described in Bloom's (1956) Taxonomy of Cognitive Development, "non-in-depth" refers to the levels of knowledge, understanding, and application (see "higher-order learning").

Oliva model: A model for curriculum development featuring a sequence of steps ranging from curriculum goals developed based on various sources of information to a final curriculum evaluation through several planning and operational phases.

Open Court Reading: A published elementary basal reading program for grades K–6 developed by SRA/McGraw-Hill. The program is designed to systematically teach decoding, comprehension, inquiry and investigation, and writing in a logical progression (Institute of Education Sciences).

Outcomes-based curriculum: Where the identification of instructional outcomes is the basis for any planning efforts, thus leading to student performance supposed to evidence the same outcomes.

Parallel Curriculum Model: The selecting of a range of "parallel" ways in which to select and design content intended to challenge learners.

Performance objectives: The expected level of student performance or proficiency as a result of engaging in an instructional activity designed to help students meet the set objective. A common element in a lesson plan (see "learning objectives").

Positive reinforcement systems: Programs designed to reward desired or acceptable student behavior by means of positive consequences to the behavior in question.

Professional development: When used in education, refers to the training that teachers take to improve practice.

Project-based learning: A system that involves students in complex and interdisciplinary authentic learning tasks that require higher-level thinking, communication, and collaborative skills, prompted by a range of formative assessment tools.

Saxon Math: A published K–12 program that relies on a gradual approach to the introduction of new mathematical concepts and skills.

"School within school": An example of school transformation or restructuring stemming from the principle that a smaller school promotes more positive interactions, leading to better student performance and overall school climate.

Short-cycle assessments: A way to measure what a student knows that is formative in nature; students do not take a lot of time to implement this measurement, thus providing teachers with data related to the progress of their students.

Society-centered curricula: A system that intends to prepare citizens to meet the needs of the society as a whole. For instance, if more engineers are needed for the economy, science and mathematics will be emphasized.

Socioeconomic status (SES): A term used by educators and social scientists to refer to a student's parent or guardian's level of education and income. The percentage of students receiving free or reduced lunch is the most common way of measuring SES in schools.

Standards-driven curriculum: An example of integrating content standards into teaching, learning, and assessment.

Stereotypes: Labels or categories applied to individuals identifying as belonging to a particular group, thus leading to isolation or discrimination.

Teacher autonomy: The freedom allowed to a teacher to make decisions about his or her practice.

Teacher-centered: Unlike student-centered instruction or curriculum, teacher-centered teaching and learning is determined by the teacher with little or any input from the students.

Theme-based schools and curriculum: A system that uses a broad theme such as fantasy around which all learning takes place. This is done to enhance the connections between content areas (curriculum coherence) and as a way to motivate students to learn.

Title I programs: Based on federal guidelines, these aim to support schools serving a high number or percentage of students coming from impoverished backgrounds by providing them with opportunities to meet the challenges of academic standards.

Tolerance: The ability to accept ideas, viewpoints, perspectives, or practices different from one's own.

Universal Design for Learning (UDL): A framework that relies on a balance between high standards and student diversity in ways that maximize individual learning.

Walker's deliberative approach: A way to plan curriculum that relies on the process of interacting among different participants based on a variety of information sources designed to support the development of a new curriculum.

REFERENCES

Bloom, B. S. (1956). *Taxonomy of educational objectives: The classification of educational goals.* New York: Susan Fauer Company.

Eisner, E. W. (1979). *The educational imagination.* Upper Saddle River, NJ: Merrill/ Prentice Hall.

Ellis, A. K. (2004). *Exemplars of curriculum theory.* Larchmont, NY: Eye on Education.

Gardner, H. (1983). *Frames of mind.* New York: Basic Books.

U.S. Department of Education Institute of Education Sciences (IES). (2008, August). *Open court reading.* Retrieved April 15, 2009, from http://ies.ed.gov/ncee/wwc/ reports/beginning_reading/open_court/

Index

About the Authors

Marius Boboc is an associate professor of education at Cleveland State University, where he teaches undergraduate courses in general methods of instruction and student assessment, as well as graduate courses in curriculum theory and classroom management. He is also the director of Student Learning Assessment at his institution. His teaching background ranges from third grade all the way up to college, in the areas of French, English as a foreign language, creative writing, and American literature. His research agenda includes postmodernism in education, effective methods of teaching, online pedagogy, and educational technology in higher education, as well as assessment, accreditation, and quality assurance in higher education. He earned his MA in teacher education from Roosevelt University in Chicago and his EdD in curriculum and instruction from the University of Northern Iowa in Cedar Falls.

R. D. Nordgren is an associate professor of urban education at Cleveland State University where he teaches a variety of undergraduate and graduate courses in both teacher education and school administration. He taught English/language arts and was a site-based administrator at the middle and high school levels in Florida. Nordgren's research interests are the PK–16 education continuum, specifically the transition from high school to university, and examining the "soft skills" needed for success in university and the globalized economy and society. He earned his PhD at the University of South Florida in interdisciplinary studies in curriculum and instruction with an emphasis on school management. Nordgren is originally from Galesburg, Illinois.